Ireland Travel Guide

Explore Hidden Gems and Local Culture with Insider Tips - Experience The Ultimate Irish Experience From Ancient Castles to Breathtaking Landscapes

Jake Fallon

© Copyright 2024 by Jake Fallon
All rights reserved

This document is geared towards providing exact and reliable information with regards to the topic and issue covered. The publication is sold with the idea that the publisher is not required to render accounting, officially permitted, or otherwise, qualified services. If advice is necessary, legal or professional, a practiced individual in the profession should be ordered.

From a Declaration of Principles which was accepted and approved equally by a Committee of the American Bar Association and a Committee of Publishers and Associations.

In no way is it legal to reproduce, duplicate, or transmit any part of this document in either electronic means or in printed format. Recording of this publication is strictly prohibited and any storage of this document is not allowed unless with written permission from the publisher. All rights reserved.

The information provided herein is stated to be truthful and consistent, in that any liability, in terms of inattention or otherwise, by any usage or abuse of any policies, processes, or directions contained within is the solitary and utter responsibility of the recipient reader. Under no circumstances will any legal responsibility or blame be held against the publisher for any reparation, damages, or monetary loss due to the information herein, either directly or indirectly.

Respective authors own all copyrights not held by the publisher.

The information herein is offered for informational purposes solely, and is universal as so. The presentation of the information is without contract or any type of guarantee assurance.

The trademarks that are used are without any consent, and the publication of the trademark is without permission or backing by the trademark owner. All trademarks and brands within this book are for clarifying purposes only and are the owned by the owners themselves, not affiliated with this document.

TABLE OF CONTENTS

Chapter 1: Introduction to Ireland 7
    1.1   A Brief History of Ireland 7
    1.2   Understanding Irish Culture 10
    1.3   Essential Travel Tips 13
    1.4   Best Times to Visit 16
    1.5   Navigating Your Journey 19

Chapter 2: Dublin – The Heart of Ireland 23
    2.1 Exploring Dublin's Historic Sites 23
    2.2 Hidden Gems in the Capital 26
    2.3 Dublin's Vibrant Nightlife 29
    2.4 Culinary Delights in Dublin 32
    2.5 Self-Guided Walking Tours 35
    2.6 Local Festivals and Events 38

Chapter 3: Ancient Castles and Ruins 43
    3.1 The Mystique of Irish Castles 43
    3.2 Top Castles to Visit 46
    3.3 Ruins with a Story 49
    3.4 Guided Tours vs. Solo Exploration 52
    3.5 Photography Tips for Castles 55
    3.6 Preservation and History 58

Chapter 4: Scenic Drives and Natural Wonders 63
    4.1 The Wild Atlantic Way 63
    4.2 The Ring of Kerry 66
    4.3 Coastal Drives and Hidden Beaches 69
    4.4 Hiking Trails and Outdoor Adventures 71
    4.5 National Parks and Wildlife 75
    4.6 Exploring the Aran Islands 78
    4.7 Local Legends and Folklore 82

Chapter 5: Connecting with Local Culture 87

5.1 Traditional Irish Music and Dance 87

5.2 Pubs and the Art of Conversation... 90

5.3 Festivals and Cultural Events.. 93

5.4 Gaelic Language and Traditions.. 96

5.5 Engaging with Locals 100

5.6 Art and Literature in Ireland.. 103

Chapter 6: Culinary Journey Through Ireland.. 108

6.1 Traditional Irish Dishes.. 108

6.2 Modern Irish Cuisine 111

6.3 Best Places to Eat 114

6.4 Local Markets and Food Festivals 117

6.5 Whiskey and Brewery Tours.. 120

Chapter 7: Exploring Ireland's Regions.. 126

7.1 The Charm of Galway 126

7.2 The Beauty of Cork and Kerry.. 128

7.3 Northern Ireland's Rich Heritage 131

7.4 The Midlands and Ancient East 134

7.5 The Undiscovered West 137

7.6 Regional Itineraries and Highlights... 140

7.7 Local Guides and Tours 142

Chapter 8: Conclusion and Further Resources 147

8.1 Reflecting on Your Journey 147

8.2 Final Tips and Farewell.. 149

BONUS 1: Essential phrases for your daily travel needs in Ireland 153

BONUS 2: Printable travel journal... 154

BONUS 3: 10 tips "that can save the day" on your Irish trip 155

CHAPTER 1: INTRODUCTION TO IRELAND

1.1   A Brief History of Ireland

Ireland's history, a tapestry woven with threads of mythology, conquest, resistance, and cultural renaissance, beckons the curious traveler to delve into its rich past. The tale begins with ancient legends, where the Tuatha Dé Danann, a race of god-like beings, inhabited the land before the arrival of the Celts. These mythological tales, passed down through generations, paint a picture of a mystical island shrouded in enchantment.

As history unfolded, the Celts emerged around 600 BC, bringing with them a unique culture and social structure. They established kingdoms, each ruled by a chieftain, and a society that revered poets, warriors, and druids. Their influence remains palpable in Ireland's language, music, and art, forming the bedrock of Irish identity.

The arrival of Christianity in the 5th century marked a transformative period in Ireland's history. St. Patrick, the patron saint, is credited with spreading the gospel across the island, replacing pagan practices with Christian teachings. This era witnessed the establishment of monastic settlements, such as Clonmacnoise and Glendalough, which became centers of learning and spiritual refuge. Monks diligently transcribed religious texts, preserving knowledge through illuminated manuscripts like the Book of Kells, an exquisite example of medieval artistry.

Viking invasions in the late 8th century brought turmoil and change to Ireland's shores. Norse settlers established coastal towns, including Dublin, Waterford, and Limerick, which flourished as trading hubs. Despite initial conflict, the Vikings eventually integrated into Irish society, leaving a lasting legacy in place names and urban development.

The Norman invasion in 1169 introduced another chapter of conquest and assimilation. With the backing of King Henry II of England, Norman forces led by Strongbow landed in Ireland, quickly establishing control over large territories. Norman architecture, characterized by imposing castles and cathedrals, began to dot the landscape, while their feudal system reshaped Irish society.

The centuries that followed were marked by a complex interplay of power struggles between Irish chieftains, Anglo-Norman lords, and the English crown. The Tudor conquest in the 16th century sought to establish greater control over Ireland, leading to the suppression of Gaelic culture and the introduction of English law and customs. The Plantation of Ulster in the early 17th century further altered the demographic and cultural landscape, as Protestant settlers from Scotland and England were encouraged to colonize the region.

Religious tensions simmered throughout the 17th and 18th centuries, culminating in the Williamite War, where Catholic and Protestant forces clashed. The Battle of the Boyne in 1690, a significant Protestant victory, cemented English dominance, yet the seeds of division were sown, laying the groundwork for future conflict.

The 19th century witnessed a wave of political and social upheaval, as movements for Irish independence gained momentum. The Act of Union in 1801, which merged the Kingdom of Ireland with Great Britain, sparked a fervent desire for self-governance. Figures like Daniel O'Connell emerged as champions of Catholic emancipation, advocating for equal rights and representation.

The Great Famine of the 1840s, a catastrophic event that decimated the population, left an indelible mark on Ireland's history. Millions faced starvation or were forced to emigrate, seeking refuge in countries like the United States, Canada, and Australia. This diaspora spread Irish culture across the globe, establishing vibrant communities that continue to cherish their heritage.

The late 19th and early 20th centuries were characterized by a renewed push for independence, as political and cultural movements sought to reclaim Ireland's identity. The Easter Rising of 1916, a pivotal moment in the struggle for freedom, saw Irish republicans rise against British rule in a bid to establish an independent Irish Republic. Although the rebellion was swiftly suppressed, it galvanized public support for the cause.

The subsequent War of Independence from 1919 to 1921, marked by guerrilla warfare and political negotiations, ultimately led to the signing of the Anglo-Irish Treaty. This agreement established the Irish Free State, granting Ireland a measure of self-governance, while Northern Ireland remained part of the United Kingdom. The treaty, however, sowed seeds of discord, resulting in a bitter civil war between pro- and anti-treaty factions.

The mid-20th century was a period of consolidation and growth for the newly formed Republic of Ireland. Economic modernization, social reforms, and cultural resurgence defined this era, as Ireland sought to carve out its place on the world stage. The nation embraced its literary heritage, with figures like W.B. Yeats, James Joyce, and Samuel Beckett garnering international acclaim.

The Troubles, a protracted conflict in Northern Ireland from the late 1960s to 1998, cast a shadow over the island. Rooted in sectarian divisions and political grievances, the violence claimed thousands of lives and left communities deeply scarred. The Good Friday Agreement in 1998, a landmark peace accord, brought an end to the hostilities, paving the way for reconciliation and cooperation.

In recent decades, Ireland has experienced unprecedented change, embracing economic growth, technological innovation, and social progress. The Celtic Tiger era of the late 20th and early 21st centuries ushered in a period of prosperity, transforming Ireland into a hub of global business and culture. This newfound confidence has fueled a renaissance of creativity, with Irish artists, musicians, and filmmakers making their mark on the international stage.

Ireland's history is a testament to resilience, adaptability, and the enduring spirit of its people. From ancient myths to modern achievements, the island's past is a source of inspiration and reflection. As you journey through Ireland, the echoes of history resonate in the landscapes, the architecture, and the vibrant culture that continues to thrive.

1.2   Understanding Irish Culture

Irish culture, an intricate mosaic of traditions, values, and artistic expressions, offers a warm embrace to anyone willing to explore its depths. At its heart lies a profound sense of community, where family ties and friendships are cherished above all. The Irish have long been celebrated for their hospitality, extending a genuine welcome to visitors and engaging them in lively conversation. This openness is not merely a social custom but a reflection of a deeply ingrained cultural ethos.

Language plays a pivotal role in shaping Irish identity. While English is predominantly spoken, the Irish language, or Gaeilge, holds a special place in the national psyche. Efforts to preserve and promote it can be seen in Gaeltacht regions, where daily life unfolds in the native tongue. This linguistic revival is a testament to the resilience of Irish culture and its determination to honor its past while embracing the future.

Music and dance are vibrant threads in the fabric of Irish culture. Traditional Irish music, characterized by its lively jigs and soulful ballads, continues to captivate audiences both at home and abroad. Instruments like the fiddle, tin whistle, and bodhrán bring melodies to life, while the haunting strains of the uilleann pipes evoke a sense of nostalgia and longing. Dance, too, plays a vital role, with the intricate footwork of Irish step dancing captivating audiences with its precision and energy. These artistic expressions serve as a bridge between generations, connecting the past with the present.

Ireland's literary heritage is another cornerstone of its cultural identity. The island has produced some of the world's most renowned writers, from the poetic prowess of W.B. Yeats to the modernist innovations of James Joyce. Literature in Ireland is not merely an art form but a means of exploring complex themes and engaging in social and political discourse. The storytelling tradition, rooted in ancient Celtic culture, endures in the modern era, with contemporary authors continuing to contribute to this rich tapestry.

Folklore and mythology are deeply embedded in the Irish consciousness, shaping the way people perceive the world around them. Tales of faeries, leprechauns, and banshees are more than mere stories; they are a reflection of the land's mystique and the people's connection to nature. These narratives have evolved over time, adapting to contemporary contexts while retaining their essence. They serve as a reminder of Ireland's ancient past and its enduring spirit of imagination.

Religion has historically played a significant role in Irish culture, with Catholicism being the predominant faith. Churches and monasteries dot the landscape, bearing witness to centuries of devotion and spiritual reflection. Religious festivals and celebrations, such as St. Patrick's Day, are not only expressions of faith but also opportunities for communal celebration and cultural pride. However, in recent years, Irish society has become more diverse and secular, reflecting broader global trends and embracing a plurality of beliefs and practices.

The art of conversation, or "the craic," is a cherished aspect of Irish culture. Whether in a bustling pub or a quiet kitchen, the Irish have a knack for storytelling and wit, weaving tales that entertain and provoke thought. This tradition of verbal artistry transcends generations, fostering connections and creating a shared sense of community. Humor often plays a central role, with a penchant for irony and satire that adds depth and nuance to everyday interactions.

Sports, too, hold a special place in Irish culture, with Gaelic games such as hurling and Gaelic football capturing the nation's passion. These indigenous sports are more than mere pastimes; they are vehicles for community engagement and local pride. The Gaelic Athletic Association (GAA) plays a pivotal role in promoting these games, ensuring that they remain an integral part of Irish cultural life. Rugby and soccer also enjoy widespread popularity, further enriching the nation's sporting landscape.

Cuisine in Ireland has undergone a renaissance in recent years, with a renewed appreciation for traditional dishes and locally sourced ingredients. From hearty stews to freshly caught seafood, Irish cuisine reflects the land's natural bounty and the creativity of its people. Culinary festivals and farmers' markets celebrate this heritage, offering visitors an opportunity to savor authentic flavors and experience the warmth of Irish hospitality.

Art and craftsmanship are integral to Irish culture, with a rich tradition of visual and decorative arts. From the intricate designs of Celtic jewelry to the vibrant colors of contemporary paintings, Irish artists draw inspiration from their surroundings and heritage. Craftsmanship is celebrated in various forms, from handwoven textiles to pottery and glasswork, showcasing the nation's creativity and skill.

Festivals and cultural events provide a platform for celebrating Irish culture in all its diversity. From the vibrant parades of St. Patrick's Day to the literary gatherings of the Dublin International Literary Festival, these events offer a window into the soul of Ireland. They bring communities together, fostering a sense of belonging and shared identity. Whether through music, dance, literature, or art, these celebrations highlight the dynamic and evolving nature of Irish culture.

The Irish diaspora, spread across the globe, plays a vital role in preserving and promoting Irish culture. These communities, while geographically distant, remain deeply connected to their roots, celebrating their heritage through cultural events, music, and storytelling. This global network serves as a testament to the enduring appeal of Irish culture and its ability to transcend borders.

In understanding Irish culture, one gains insight into the values, traditions, and artistic expressions that define this remarkable island. It is a culture that embraces its past while looking toward the future, celebrating diversity and creativity in all its forms. As you immerse yourself in the richness of Irish culture, you become a part of its ongoing story, woven into the tapestry of a land that cherishes its heritage and welcomes the world with open arms.

1.3   Essential Travel Tips

Planning a journey to Ireland is an exciting endeavor, filled with the promise of breathtaking landscapes, rich history, and vibrant culture. To ensure your trip is as smooth and enjoyable as possible, a few essential travel tips can make all the difference. With a bit of preparation and insight, you'll be ready to embrace the full Irish experience.

When it comes to travel logistics, Ireland's compact size is a blessing. The country's excellent transport network makes it easy to hop from one scenic destination to another. Whether you choose to rent a car for a more personalized journey or rely on public transport, understanding the options available is key. Driving in Ireland can be a thrilling adventure, with its winding country roads and stunning coastal routes. However, it's important to remember that driving is on the left side, and rural roads can be narrow. For those who prefer not to drive, the public transport system, including trains and buses, is reliable and connects major cities and towns efficiently.

Packing for Ireland requires a bit of forethought, given the island's famously unpredictable weather. Layers are your best friend, allowing you to adjust to sudden changes in temperature. A good waterproof jacket is indispensable, as rain showers can occur at any time. Comfortable walking shoes are a must, especially if you plan to explore the many hiking trails and historic sites. While Ireland is generally a safe destination, it's wise to take standard travel precautions, such as securing your belongings and being aware of your surroundings.

Currency in Ireland is the Euro, except in Northern Ireland, where the British Pound is used. Credit and debit cards are widely accepted, but it's always handy to have a small amount of cash for smaller establishments, rural areas, or tips. ATMs are readily accessible, and many offer competitive exchange rates, making them a convenient option for withdrawing local currency.

Accommodation in Ireland caters to a wide range of preferences and budgets. From luxurious castles and boutique hotels to cozy bed and breakfasts and charming guesthouses, there's something for everyone. Booking in advance is recommended, particularly during peak tourist seasons and in popular areas. Staying in a local B&B can enhance your cultural experience, offering a glimpse into Irish hospitality and providing a chance to connect with warm-hearted hosts.

Connectivity is essential for modern travelers, and Ireland is well-equipped to meet these needs. Wi-Fi is widely available in urban centers, hotels, and cafes, allowing you to stay connected with ease. If you plan to use your mobile phone extensively, consider purchasing a local SIM card for better rates on calls and data. This can be especially useful for navigating with GPS or staying in touch with loved ones back home.

One of the most rewarding aspects of traveling in Ireland is the opportunity to engage with the local culture. The Irish are renowned for their friendliness and love of conversation, so don't hesitate to strike up a chat with locals. Whether you're in a bustling pub or a quiet village, you'll likely find someone eager to share a story or offer a recommendation. Embrace the chance to participate in cultural events, attend live music performances, or join a traditional dance session. These experiences provide invaluable insights into the heart of Irish life.

Food is another delightful way to immerse yourself in Irish culture. While traditional dishes like Irish stew and soda bread are must-tries, don't miss the chance to explore the burgeoning modern culinary scene. From farm-to-table eateries to innovative chefs putting a fresh spin on classics, Ireland's food landscape is diverse and exciting. Sampling local produce at farmers' markets or indulging in a seafood feast along the coast are experiences that will tantalize your taste buds and leave a lasting impression.

Nature lovers will find endless opportunities to connect with Ireland's stunning landscapes. Whether you're traversing the rugged cliffs of the Wild Atlantic Way, hiking in the lush national parks, or exploring the serene beauty of the lakes and mountains, the natural world here is both awe-inspiring and accessible. Be sure to respect the environment, following the Leave No Trace principles to preserve Ireland's natural heritage for future generations.

Cultural etiquette in Ireland is generally relaxed, but a few pointers can enhance your interactions. Punctuality is appreciated, especially in formal settings, though social gatherings tend to be more flexible. Tipping is customary in restaurants and cafes, typically around 10-15% for good service. While the Irish are known for their wit and humor, it's wise to be mindful of sensitive topics such as politics or religion, especially with those you don't know well.

Finally, embracing spontaneity can lead to some of the most memorable travel experiences. While it's important to have a plan, allowing room for unexpected detours or discoveries can open up a world of possibilities. Whether you stumble upon a hidden beach, join an impromptu music session, or receive a local's invitation to a family gathering, these moments often become the highlights of your journey.

Traveling in Ireland is a rich and rewarding experience, offering a blend of natural beauty, cultural depth, and warm hospitality. By preparing with these essential tips in mind, you'll be well-equipped to embark on an unforgettable adventure, discovering the myriad charms of this captivating island.

1.4 Best Times to Visit

Choosing the best time to visit Ireland can greatly enhance your travel experience, as the island offers distinct charms and activities throughout the year. Each season brings its own unique appeal, reflecting the dynamic character of Ireland's landscapes and culture. Understanding the nuances of each period can help you tailor your journey to match your interests and preferences.

Spring, from March to May, is a delightful time to witness Ireland waking from its winter slumber. The countryside becomes a tapestry of vibrant greens as new growth emerges, and wildflowers burst into color across the hills and valleys. This season is perfect for nature enthusiasts who wish to explore the island's national parks and gardens, with pleasant temperatures averaging between 10 to 15 degrees Celsius (50 to 59 degrees Fahrenheit). Spring also heralds the beginning of the festival season, with St. Patrick's Day on March 17th offering a lively celebration of Irish culture, complete with parades, music, and plenty of craic. It's a time when cities and towns come alive with festivities, providing a perfect opportunity to soak in the local atmosphere.

Summer, from June to August, is peak tourist season, and for good reason. The days are long, with up to 18 hours of daylight, allowing you to make the most of your exploration. Average temperatures range from 15 to 20 degrees Celsius (59 to 68 degrees Fahrenheit), making it an ideal time for outdoor activities such as hiking, cycling, and exploring Ireland's stunning beaches. Coastal areas, like the Wild Atlantic Way, offer breathtaking views and opportunities for water sports. Summer is also synonymous with a vibrant festival scene, from music and arts to food and cultural events, such as the Galway International Arts Festival and the Kilkenny Arts Festival. However, it's important to note that the popularity of this season means that accommodations can fill up quickly, so booking in advance is advised to secure your preferred choice.

Autumn, spanning September to November, is a time when the hustle and bustle of summer fades, and Ireland's landscapes take on a warm, golden hue. This season is perfect for those who prefer a quieter experience, with fewer crowds and a more relaxed pace. Temperatures remain mild, averaging between 10 to 15 degrees Celsius (50 to 59 degrees Fahrenheit), making it a comfortable time for exploring Ireland's historic sites and vibrant cities. Autumn also marks the harvest season, offering a chance to indulge in fresh, local produce at food festivals and markets. The changing foliage adds an enchanting quality to the countryside, providing a picturesque backdrop for scenic drives and leisurely walks. The Dublin Theatre Festival, held in late September to early October, is a highlight for culture lovers, showcasing an array of performances and productions.

Winter, from December to February, unveils a different side of Ireland, one that is cozy and intimate. While temperatures can dip to between 3 to 8 degrees Celsius (37 to 46 degrees Fahrenheit), the weather is generally milder than other parts of Europe, with occasional frosts and rare snowfall in lowland areas. This season offers a chance to experience Ireland's rich cultural heritage in a more tranquil setting. The festive season brings a magical atmosphere, with Christmas markets, twinkling lights, and traditional music adding warmth to the winter chill. The New Year is celebrated with enthusiasm, particularly in cities like Dublin, where the New Year's Festival features a variety of events and activities. Winter is also an ideal time to explore indoor attractions, such as museums, galleries, and historic houses, without the crowds.

Regardless of the season, Ireland's weather can be unpredictable, with rain showers possible at any time of year. Packing a good waterproof jacket and layers is always advisable, ensuring you're prepared for sudden changes in weather. The island's climate is maritime, influenced by the Atlantic Ocean, which brings mild temperatures and frequent rainfall, contributing to Ireland's lush, green landscapes.

Each season offers unique experiences and opportunities, allowing you to tailor your visit to suit your interests. Whether you're drawn to the vibrant energy of summer festivals, the tranquil beauty of autumn landscapes, the festive charm of winter, or the fresh vitality of spring, Ireland welcomes you with open arms. By understanding the best times to visit, you can make the most of your journey, discovering the myriad wonders that this enchanting island has to offer.

1.5 Navigating Your Journey

Embarking on a journey through Ireland is akin to stepping into a living storybook, where each chapter unfolds with new adventures and discoveries. Navigating this enchanting land requires a blend of planning and spontaneity, ensuring you capture both the must-see sights and the hidden gems that make Ireland unique.

Understanding your transportation options is crucial for a seamless journey. Ireland's compact size and well-developed transport infrastructure make it relatively easy to travel between destinations. Renting a car is a popular choice, offering the freedom to explore at your own pace and venture off the beaten path. With the steering wheel on the right side and driving on the left, it can be an adjustment for those used to different systems, but it quickly becomes second nature. The views from the road are often spectacular, with the Wild Atlantic Way and the Ring of Kerry offering some of the most scenic drives imaginable.

For those who prefer not to drive, public transport is a viable alternative. Ireland's train network, operated by Irish Rail, connects major cities and towns, providing a comfortable and efficient way to see the country. Trains are an excellent option for longer distances, offering views of the countryside and a chance to relax between destinations. For more localized travel, buses are widely available, with services like Bus Éireann and private operators covering extensive routes. In cities like Dublin, the Luas tram and DART train offer convenient ways to navigate urban areas.

Cycling enthusiasts will find Ireland a welcoming destination, with numerous bike trails and rental options available. Whether you're exploring the lush landscapes of County Clare or the rugged terrain of Connemara, cycling provides an intimate way to experience Ireland's natural beauty. Many towns and cities have invested in cycling infrastructure, making it an increasingly popular choice for both locals and visitors.

Once you've settled on your mode of transport, understanding the landscape and geography of Ireland aids in route planning. The island is divided into four provinces—Leinster, Munster, Connacht, and Ulster—each offering distinct characteristics and attractions. Leinster, home to the capital city of Dublin, is a vibrant mix of urban and rural, with historic sites and cultural landmarks. Munster boasts dramatic coastal scenery and charming towns, such as Cork and Killarney, while Connacht is known for its rugged beauty and traditional Irish culture. Ulster, which includes Northern Ireland, offers a wealth of history and stunning landscapes, including the Giant's Causeway and the Antrim Coast.

Accommodation choices can greatly influence your travel experience. Ireland offers a diverse range of options, from luxury hotels and historic castles to cozy bed and breakfasts and self-catering cottages. Booking in advance, particularly during peak seasons, ensures you have a place to rest after a day of exploration. Staying in a local B&B not only supports the community but also provides an opportunity to engage with locals and gain insider tips. Many hosts are eager to share their knowledge and recommend attractions that might not be on the typical tourist itinerary.

Dining in Ireland is a culinary journey in itself, with an emphasis on fresh, locally sourced ingredients. Traditional Irish dishes are a must-try, but don't shy away from the innovative modern cuisine that reflects Ireland's evolving food scene. Local pubs often serve hearty meals, alongside a pint of Guinness or a glass of Irish whiskey, allowing you to savor the flavors of the land. Exploring regional specialties, from seafood in coastal towns to artisanal cheeses and produce, deepens your connection to the places you visit.

Engaging with Ireland's culture and people is integral to navigating your journey. The Irish are famously friendly and welcoming, often eager to share a story or offer assistance. Participating in local events, whether it's a music session in a pub or a community festival, enriches your experience and provides insight into the social fabric of the region. Embrace the opportunity to learn a few phrases in the Irish language, as a simple "Dia dhuit" (hello) can open doors and hearts.

Technology can be a helpful companion during your travels. Apps for navigation, accommodation booking, and local information can streamline your journey, providing real-time updates and recommendations. However, balancing digital tools with a sense of adventure and exploration is key. Allow yourself the freedom to wander and discover unexpected delights, as some of the best experiences come from unplanned moments.

Respecting Ireland's natural and cultural heritage is essential. The landscapes that captivate visitors are fragile ecosystems, and preserving them for future generations requires mindful travel. Adhering to Leave No Trace principles, respecting wildlife, and supporting local conservation efforts ensure that Ireland's beauty remains intact. Similarly, engaging with cultural sites and traditions with sensitivity and respect enriches your understanding and appreciation of Ireland's rich heritage.

As you navigate your journey through Ireland, the interplay of preparation and spontaneity creates a dynamic and fulfilling travel experience. By embracing the rhythms of local life, exploring beyond the well-trodden paths, and connecting with the people and places, you embark on a voyage that is as much about discovery as it is about understanding. Ireland's story is one of resilience, creativity, and warmth, and your journey becomes a part of this ever-evolving narrative.

CHAPTER 2: DUBLIN – THE HEART OF IRELAND

2.1 Exploring Dublin's Historic Sites

Dublin, a city where history whispers from every cobblestone and echoes through its ancient architecture, offers a captivating tapestry of stories waiting to be discovered. As the capital of Ireland, Dublin boasts a rich historical heritage that draws visitors from across the globe. To truly appreciate the essence of this vibrant city, one must wander through its historic sites, each a testament to its storied past and cultural evolution.

Begin your journey at Dublin Castle, a formidable structure that stands as a symbol of the city's resilience and transformation. Originally established as a medieval fortress by King John of England in the early 13th century, the castle has played a central role in Ireland's history. It served as the seat of British rule in Ireland for centuries before becoming a key site for the newly independent Irish state. Today, visitors can explore its opulent state apartments, the Gothic Chapel Royal, and the remnants of medieval towers, delving into the layers of history that have shaped this iconic landmark.

Just a stone's throw from the castle lies Christ Church Cathedral, one of Dublin's most magnificent medieval structures. Founded in the 11th century, the cathedral's stunning architecture and rich history make it a must-visit destination. The crypt, which dates back to the 12th century, is the largest in Ireland and houses fascinating artifacts, including the mummified remains of a cat and a rat, affectionately known as "Tom and Jerry." The cathedral's exquisite interior, with its soaring arches and intricate stained glass, offers a serene space for reflection and appreciation of its historical significance.

St. Patrick's Cathedral, Ireland's largest church, is another architectural gem that stands as a testament to Dublin's ecclesiastical heritage. Built in honor of Ireland's patron saint, St. Patrick, the cathedral was founded in 1191 and has since been a focal point of religious and cultural life in the city. The writer Jonathan Swift, author of "Gulliver's Travels," served as dean of the cathedral in the early 18th century and is buried within its walls. A visit to St. Patrick's offers not only a chance to admire its Gothic splendor but also to explore its rich history and connection to Ireland's literary tradition.

Trinity College Dublin, Ireland's oldest university, is a beacon of learning and history. Founded in 1592 by Queen Elizabeth I, the college's historic campus is home to the world-renowned Book of Kells. This illuminated manuscript, created by Celtic monks around the year 800, is a masterpiece of medieval art and a testament to Ireland's early Christian heritage. The Long Room of the Old Library, with its stunning barrel-vaulted ceiling and collection of over 200,000 ancient books, is a sight to behold and a haven for bibliophiles.

A stroll through the cobbled streets of Temple Bar offers a glimpse into Dublin's past and present. This vibrant cultural quarter, known for its lively atmosphere and bustling nightlife, is steeped in history. The area once served as a Viking settlement before evolving into a hub of commerce and trade in the medieval period. Today, Temple Bar is a center for arts and culture, with galleries, theaters, and music venues offering a diverse range of experiences. As you wander its streets, you'll encounter historic buildings and hidden courtyards that speak to the area's rich history.

The General Post Office (GPO) on O'Connell Street is a landmark of Dublin's modern history, playing a pivotal role in the 1916 Easter Rising. This event marked a turning point in Ireland's struggle for independence from British rule. The GPO's grand neoclassical façade bears the scars of the rebellion, with bullet holes still visible in its columns. Inside, an interpretive center provides insight into the events of the Rising and its impact on Ireland's path to independence.

Visiting the GPO offers a profound connection to the nation's fight for freedom and sovereignty.

Kilmainham Gaol, a former prison turned museum, offers a somber yet important perspective on Ireland's turbulent history. Opened in 1796, the gaol housed many of Ireland's political prisoners, including leaders of the 1916 Easter Rising. The prison's stark cells and haunting corridors tell the stories of those who fought for Irish independence and suffered the consequences. Guided tours provide a poignant narrative of the individuals who shaped Ireland's destiny, making it a deeply moving experience for visitors.

The National Museum of Ireland, with its multiple branches across Dublin, offers a comprehensive exploration of the country's rich cultural heritage. From archaeology to decorative arts, the museum's collections provide a window into Ireland's past, from prehistoric times to the present day. The Archaeology branch, located on Kildare Street, is home to treasures such as the Ardagh Chalice and the Tara Brooch, while the Decorative Arts and History branch at Collins Barracks showcases Ireland's social and military history.

Phoenix Park, one of the largest enclosed public parks in Europe, offers a tranquil escape from the hustle and bustle of the city. Established in the 17th century, the park is home to Áras an Uachtaráin, the official residence of the President of Ireland, as well as Dublin Zoo and a herd of wild deer. The park's vast expanses of greenery and historic monuments provide a serene setting for leisurely strolls and picnics, offering a glimpse into Dublin's natural and cultural landscape.

As you delve into Dublin's historic sites, you'll uncover the layers of history that have shaped this dynamic city. Each landmark and monument offers a unique perspective on Ireland's past, inviting you to explore the stories and events that have left an indelible mark on its cultural identity. From medieval cathedrals to revolutionary sites, Dublin's rich history is a testament to the resilience and creativity of its people, offering a captivating journey through time.

2.2 Hidden Gems in the Capital

Dublin, while renowned for its iconic landmarks and vibrant city life, holds a treasure trove of lesser-known wonders waiting to be discovered. These hidden gems, often overshadowed by more famous attractions, offer an intimate glimpse into the soul of the city. Each spot tells a story, revealing layers of history, culture, and creativity that make Dublin truly unique.

One such gem is the Marsh's Library, a haven for bibliophiles and history enthusiasts alike. Established in 1707, it stands as the first public library in Ireland and remains remarkably unchanged since its inception. Tucked away behind St. Patrick's Cathedral, the library is a quiet sanctuary filled with over 25,000 rare books and manuscripts. Its beautifully preserved interior, with oak bookcases and intricate ironwork, transports visitors back to the Enlightenment era. Among its notable visitors was Jonathan Swift, the author of "Gulliver's Travels," who perused its collections. Wandering through the narrow aisles, one can't help but feel a connection to the literary greats who once studied in this very spot.

The Little Museum of Dublin, located on St. Stephen's Green, offers another intimate experience. This charming museum, housed in a Georgian townhouse, provides a snapshot of life in Dublin over the past century. Through a collection of artifacts donated by Dubliners, the museum tells the story of the city through the eyes of its residents. From U2 memorabilia to pieces from the 1916 Easter Rising, each exhibit is a testament to Dublin's vibrant cultural history. The personal anecdotes shared by the museum's guides add depth and authenticity, making each visit a unique journey through time.

For those seeking a touch of whimsy, the National Leprechaun Museum offers a delightful escape into the world of Irish folklore. Situated in the heart of the city, this interactive museum invites visitors to explore the myths and legends that have shaped Ireland's cultural identity. Through storytelling and immersive exhibits, the museum brings to life the tales of leprechauns, fairies, and other mythical creatures. It's a place where imagination reigns, providing a light-hearted yet insightful look into the folklore that continues to influence Irish culture.

Iveagh Gardens, often referred to as Dublin's "Secret Garden," is a tranquil oasis hidden in plain sight. While St. Stephen's Green and Phoenix Park draw larger crowds, Iveagh Gardens remains a peaceful retreat for those in the know. Originally designed in the 19th century, the gardens feature a unique blend of landscape styles, including a rustic grotto, a sunken lawn, and a yew maze. Its serene atmosphere and lush greenery make it an ideal spot for a leisurely stroll or a quiet moment of reflection amidst the city's hustle and bustle.

Another enchanting escape can be found at the Chester Beatty Library, located within the grounds of Dublin Castle. This award-winning museum and library houses an exquisite collection of manuscripts, rare books, and artifacts from across the globe. The collections span centuries and continents, offering a fascinating glimpse into the world's artistic and cultural heritage. Visitors can marvel at treasures such as ancient Egyptian papyri, illuminated Qur'ans, and Japanese scrolls, each piece a masterpiece in its own right. The library's tranquil setting, combined with its world-class exhibitions, makes it a must-visit destination for art and history lovers.

For a taste of Dublin's culinary creativity, venture to the Fumbally Stables. This hidden gem in the Liberties area is a hub for food innovation and community gatherings. The stables host a variety of events, from pop-up dinners to workshops and markets, all centered around sustainable and locally sourced produce. It's a place where creativity and community intersect, offering visitors a chance to engage with Dublin's dynamic food scene in an authentic and interactive setting.

Music enthusiasts will find a hidden treasure in the Cobblestone Pub, located in the historic Smithfield district. Known as one of Dublin's best spots for traditional Irish music, the Cobblestone is a haven for musicians and music lovers alike. The pub's unassuming exterior belies its vibrant interior, where the sounds of fiddles, flutes, and bodhráns fill the air. Regular sessions provide an authentic experience of Ireland's musical heritage, with both seasoned musicians and newcomers joining in the lively tunes. It's a place where the spirit of Irish music thrives, offering an unforgettable experience for those lucky enough to stumble upon it.

The Forty Foot, a historic bathing area located in Sandycove, offers a unique experience for those willing to brave the chilly waters of Dublin Bay. Popularized by James Joyce's "Ulysses," the Forty Foot has been a favorite spot for sea swimming for over 250 years. Its rugged cliffs and invigorating waters provide a refreshing escape from city life, attracting both locals and adventurous visitors. Whether you choose to dive in or simply enjoy the spectacular views, a visit to the Forty Foot is a quintessential Dublin experience.

Lastly, the vibrant street art scene in Dublin offers a hidden yet ever-evolving canvas of creativity. From the alleys of Temple Bar to the walls of the Liberties, Dublin's urban landscape is adorned with colorful murals and thought-provoking graffiti. These works of art reflect the city's dynamic spirit and provide a visual narrative of its contemporary culture. Exploring Dublin's street art is like embarking on a treasure hunt, with each piece offering a glimpse into the city's soul and the voices of its artists.

These hidden gems, each with its own story and charm, enrich the tapestry of Dublin's cultural landscape. They invite you to step off the beaten path and discover the lesser-known wonders that make Dublin truly special. As you wander through these unique sites, you'll uncover the layers of history, creativity, and community that define this captivating city. Dublin's hidden gems offer a journey of discovery, inviting you to see the city through the eyes of those who call it home.

2.3 Dublin's Vibrant Nightlife

As the sun dips below the horizon, Dublin transforms into a city pulsating with life, offering a nightlife experience that is as diverse as it is vibrant. The Irish capital has long been renowned for its rich musical heritage and lively pub culture, making it a must-visit destination for those who wish to experience the true essence of Irish hospitality after dark. Dublin's nightlife scene is an eclectic mix of traditional and contemporary, catering to a wide range of tastes and preferences.

At the heart of Dublin's nightlife is its legendary pub scene, where the warm glow of candlelight and the comforting hum of conversation welcome patrons from near and far. The Temple Bar area, though bustling with tourists, offers an authentic introduction to Dublin's pub culture. Here, you can find iconic establishments such as The Temple Bar Pub itself, known for its extensive whiskey collection and nightly live music sessions. Traditional Irish tunes spill out onto the cobbled streets, enticing passersby to join in the revelry and dance the night away.

For a more intimate setting, venture to The Long Hall, a Victorian-era pub that has retained its old-world charm. With its ornate mirrors, dark wooden interiors, and inviting atmosphere, it offers a glimpse into Dublin's past while providing the perfect backdrop for a quiet pint and engaging conversation. Another beloved institution is Mulligan's, famed for its perfectly poured pints of Guinness and storied history dating back to 1782. Locals and visitors alike gather here to enjoy the simple pleasures of good company and great beer.

Dublin's live music scene extends beyond traditional Irish folk, encompassing an array of genres and styles. The city is home to numerous venues that host both emerging and established artists, making it a hub for music lovers. Whelan's, on Wexford Street, is a legendary venue that has seen performances by the likes of Ed Sheeran and Arctic Monkeys. With its intimate setting and eclectic lineup, it offers an unforgettable experience for those seeking live music in the heart of Dublin.

For jazz enthusiasts, The Sugar Club on Leeson Street offers an elegant yet relaxed atmosphere with a regular lineup of jazz, soul, and funk performances. Its art deco interior and comfortable seating make it an ideal spot for enjoying a night of smooth tunes and creative cocktails. The Button Factory, located in the heart of Temple Bar, is another popular venue that hosts a diverse range of acts, from indie bands to electronic DJs, ensuring there is always something exciting happening on any given night.

Dublin's nightlife is not limited to music and pubs; the city also boasts an impressive array of bars and clubs that cater to a variety of tastes. Vintage Cocktail Club, tucked away behind an unassuming door in Temple Bar, transports patrons to a bygone era with its speakeasy vibe and expertly crafted cocktails. The dimly lit interior, complete with plush seating and vintage décor, creates an intimate and sophisticated atmosphere perfect for a night of indulgence.

For those in search of a more contemporary experience, Peruke & Periwig offers a unique blend of history and modernity. This stylish bar, located in a Georgian townhouse, is known for its innovative cocktails inspired by Dublin's rich past. Each drink on the menu tells a story, offering a taste of the city's heritage with a modern twist. The upstairs lounge, with its cozy ambiance and eclectic playlist, provides a chic setting for a memorable night out.

Dance enthusiasts will find no shortage of clubs to keep them moving until the early hours. Copper Face Jacks, affectionately known as "Coppers," is a Dublin institution, beloved for its lively dance floors and friendly atmosphere. Attracting a diverse crowd, it's a place where locals and visitors alike come together to celebrate the joy of music and dance. Alternatively, Opium on Wexford Street offers a fusion of clubbing and dining, with its Asian-inspired décor and a lineup of DJs that keep the energy high throughout the night.

For a more alternative scene, The Workman's Club on Wellington Quay offers a laid-back vibe and an eclectic mix of music and events. Whether you're in the mood for a live gig, an indie DJ set, or a comedy night, this venue has something for everyone, making it a favorite among Dublin's creative crowd. Its quirky interiors and welcoming atmosphere make it the perfect place to unwind and enjoy a night of entertainment.

Dublin's nightlife also embraces the arts, with numerous theaters and performance spaces offering evening entertainment. The Abbey Theatre, Ireland's national theater, showcases a diverse range of productions, from classic Irish plays to contemporary works. A night at the theater offers a different kind of cultural experience, providing insight into Ireland's rich literary and artistic heritage.

For those who prefer a more interactive experience, Laughter Lounge on Eden Quay offers a night of comedy and camaraderie. With a lineup of both local and international comedians, it's a place where laughter reigns supreme, offering a lighthearted escape from the everyday.

As the night unfolds, Dublin's vibrant nightlife offers an array of experiences that cater to every taste and preference. From the traditional warmth of its pubs to the modern allure of its bars and clubs, the city invites you to immerse yourself in its lively atmosphere and forge unforgettable memories. Whether you're seeking the soulful strains of traditional Irish music, the rhythm of a dance floor, or the intrigue of a hidden speakeasy, Dublin's nightlife promises an adventure that will leave you longing for more.

2.4 Culinary Delights in Dublin

Dublin, a city where history and modernity coexist with ease, offers an enticing array of culinary experiences that mirror its vibrant cultural tapestry. From traditional Irish fare to innovative contemporary cuisine, the capital's food scene is a testament to its evolving identity, blending time-honored recipes with global influences. For those eager to explore Dublin's culinary delights, the city presents a feast that caters to every palate, promising a journey rich in flavors, aromas, and textures.

Start your exploration with a hearty Irish breakfast, a beloved staple that offers a taste of tradition on a plate. Typically served with bacon, sausages, black and white pudding, eggs, and tomatoes, this filling meal is often accompanied by soda bread or toast. Many cafés and restaurants across the city serve this classic dish, but for an authentic experience, try a local favorite like The Woollen Mills, where the breakfast is prepared with locally sourced ingredients and served in a cozy setting overlooking the River Liffey.

Dublin's food markets offer a treasure trove of fresh produce, artisanal products, and street food that highlight the city's dynamic food culture. The Temple Bar Food Market, held every Saturday, is a vibrant hub where vendors showcase organic vegetables, handmade cheeses, and freshly baked goods. Here, you can sample a range of local delicacies, from smoked salmon to Irish farmhouse cheeses, as you meander through stalls brimming with culinary delights. Similarly, the

Dublin Flea Market, located in Newmarket Square, combines food, crafts, and vintage finds, providing a unique opportunity to taste and discover Dublin's creative spirit.

Seafood lovers will find Dublin a haven for oceanic treats, thanks to its coastal location and rich maritime heritage. The city's proximity to the sea ensures that fresh seafood is always on the menu, from succulent oysters to tender lobster. Visit Klaw, a tiny seafood shack in Temple Bar, where you can savor freshly shucked oysters, crab claws, and seafood chowder, all served with a casual flair. For a more refined dining experience, head to The Seafood Bar by Wrights of Howth, which offers a sophisticated menu featuring the finest catches from the Irish coast.

No culinary journey in Dublin would be complete without indulging in traditional Irish stew, a dish that embodies the warmth and comfort of home cooking. Made with tender lamb or beef, potatoes, carrots, and onions, this hearty stew is perfect for warming up on a chilly day. Many pubs and restaurants serve their own versions, but The Brazen Head, Dublin's oldest pub, is renowned for its classic take on this beloved dish. Enjoy a steaming bowl in the pub's historic setting, where the walls echo tales of the past.

For those with a sweet tooth, Dublin offers an array of delightful treats that showcase its rich baking tradition. Traditional Irish scones, often enjoyed with clotted cream and jam, are a must-try, and Queen of Tarts in Dame Street is famed for its freshly baked goods and charming atmosphere. The café's selection of cakes, tarts, and pastries, made with locally sourced ingredients, provides a perfect excuse to indulge in a leisurely afternoon tea.

Dublin's culinary landscape also reflects its multicultural influences, with a diverse range of international cuisines available throughout the city. In the heart of Dublin, you can find everything from authentic Italian pizzerias to aromatic Indian curry houses. For a taste of the Middle East, head to Shouk in Drumcondra, where vibrant dishes like falafel, shakshuka, and lamb kofta are served in a relaxed and welcoming environment. The city's multicultural offerings ensure that diners can embark on a global culinary journey without ever leaving Dublin.

For those seeking cutting-edge cuisine, Dublin's fine dining scene offers innovative menus that push the boundaries of traditional flavors. Michelin-starred restaurants such as Chapter One and L'Ecrivain are known for their creative dishes that showcase the best of Irish produce, prepared with modern techniques and artistic presentation. These establishments provide an unforgettable dining experience, where each dish is a work of art that tantalizes the senses.

Dublin's vibrant café culture is another highlight, with numerous coffee shops offering expertly brewed beverages and cozy atmospheres perfect for relaxing and people-watching. 3FE, a pioneer in the city's specialty coffee scene, is a must-visit for coffee aficionados. With its focus on quality and sustainability, this café serves some of the finest coffee in Dublin, alongside a selection of delicious pastries and light bites. Whether you're seeking a quiet spot to unwind or a lively hub to meet friends, Dublin's cafés provide a welcoming space for all.

The city's burgeoning craft beer scene offers a refreshing alternative to traditional Irish pubs, with microbreweries and taprooms showcasing a range of locally brewed ales, stouts, and lagers. At The Porterhouse, Ireland's first craft brewery, you can sample a variety of unique brews, from their award-winning Plain Porter to seasonal specials. The lively atmosphere and knowledgeable staff make it an ideal spot for both beer enthusiasts and newcomers to explore the world of craft brewing.

Dublin's culinary offerings extend beyond the plate, with food festivals and events celebrating the city's diverse flavors and innovative chefs. The annual Taste of Dublin festival, held in the picturesque Iveagh Gardens, brings together top chefs, restaurants, and food producers for a weekend of gourmet experiences, cooking demonstrations, and tastings. It's a vibrant celebration of Dublin's food culture, providing an opportunity to discover new flavors and meet the people behind the city's thriving culinary scene.

As you navigate Dublin's culinary delights, you'll discover a city that embraces both its traditions and its future, offering a rich tapestry of flavors that reflect its diverse heritage and innovative spirit. Each meal, market, and café tells a story, inviting you to savor the essence of Dublin through its food. Whether you're indulging in a classic Irish dish, exploring international flavors, or sipping a perfectly brewed coffee, Dublin's culinary scene promises a journey of taste and discovery that will leave a lasting impression.

2.5 Self-Guided Walking Tours

Wandering through Dublin on foot offers a unique opportunity to uncover the city's hidden corners and immerse oneself in its rich history and culture. Self-guided walking tours provide the flexibility to explore at your own pace, allowing for spontaneous discoveries and personal connections with the city. With its compact size and pedestrian-friendly streets, Dublin is perfect for those who wish to experience its charm and character up close.

Begin your exploration in the heart of the city at O'Connell Street, a bustling thoroughfare renowned for its historical significance and iconic landmarks. As you stroll down the wide boulevard, take in the sight of the General Post Office, an imposing neoclassical building that played a central role in the 1916 Easter Rising. Pause to admire the Spire of Dublin, a striking contemporary monument that reaches skyward, a symbol of the city's modern identity. As you continue along

O'Connell Street, you'll pass statues commemorating figures from Ireland's storied past, each with its own tale to tell.

Cross the River Liffey via the pedestrian-friendly Ha'penny Bridge, a charming cast-iron structure that has connected the north and south sides of Dublin since 1816. The bridge, with its iconic arches and decorative lamps, offers picturesque views of the river and the city's skyline. Once across, you'll find yourself in the lively Temple Bar district, where cobblestone streets and colorful facades invite exploration. Although known for its vibrant nightlife, Temple Bar is also a hub of arts and culture, with galleries, theaters, and street performers adding to its eclectic atmosphere.

From Temple Bar, make your way to Trinity College Dublin, an oasis of tranquility amidst the city's bustle. Founded in 1592, the historic campus is home to the renowned Book of Kells, a stunning illuminated manuscript dating back to the 9th century. As you wander the college's grounds, take a moment to linger in the Long Room of the Old Library, a breathtaking space lined with ancient books and busts of literary greats. The serene ambiance and architectural beauty make it a must-visit stop on your walking tour.

Leaving Trinity College, head towards Grafton Street, Dublin's premier shopping thoroughfare. Here, the lively atmosphere is enhanced by the sounds of buskers performing along the street, offering a soundtrack to your stroll. As you meander past high-end boutiques and charming shops, consider stopping for a coffee or a sweet treat at one of the many cafés that line the street. Grafton Street is an ideal place to people-watch and soak in the city's vibrant energy.

At the end of Grafton Street lies St. Stephen's Green, a lush public park that provides a welcome respite from urban life. The park's manicured gardens, tranquil lakes, and meandering pathways offer a peaceful setting for a leisurely walk or a moment of reflection. As you explore its 22 acres, you'll encounter statues and monuments dedicated to notable figures from Irish history, each contributing to the park's rich narrative.

From St. Stephen's Green, continue your journey to the nearby Merrion Square, one of Dublin's most beautiful Georgian squares. The square's elegant red-brick townhouses and landscaped gardens provide a glimpse into the city's architectural heritage. Stop by the statue of Oscar Wilde, a beloved Irish writer, which captures his likeness in a playful pose. The park's tranquil ambiance is complemented by the vibrant art displays that line its railings, showcasing the talent of local artists.

A short walk from Merrion Square leads you to the National Gallery of Ireland, home to an impressive collection of art spanning the centuries. Admission is free, allowing you to explore masterpieces by renowned artists such as Caravaggio and Vermeer, as well as works by celebrated Irish painters. The gallery's light-filled spaces and diverse exhibitions offer an enriching cultural experience, providing insight into Ireland's artistic legacy.

After indulging in art, make your way to Dublin Castle, a historic site that has played a pivotal role in the city's history. Originally constructed in the 13th century, the castle has undergone numerous transformations over the centuries, reflecting the changing tides of Irish history. Within its walls, you'll find the State Apartments, the Chapel Royal, and the remnants of medieval towers, each offering a glimpse into the past. The castle's picturesque gardens provide a serene backdrop for reflection, connecting you to the city's heritage.

As your self-guided walking tour draws to a close, consider ending your journey at Christ Church Cathedral, one of Dublin's most iconic landmarks. This stunning medieval cathedral, with its soaring arches and intricate stained glass windows, stands as a testament to the city's ecclesiastical history. The crypt, dating back to the 12th century, houses fascinating artifacts and exhibitions that delve into the cathedral's storied past. Its serene interior provides a moment of tranquility, a fitting conclusion to your exploration of Dublin's rich tapestry.

Embarking on a self-guided walking tour of Dublin allows you to connect with the city in a deeply personal way, uncovering its stories and secrets at your own pace. Each step reveals a new layer of history, culture, and charm, inviting you to become a part of Dublin's ongoing narrative. As you wander the streets, you'll find that the city is more than just a collection of landmarks; it's a living, breathing entity, brimming with life and character. Through your journey, you'll forge a deeper connection to Dublin, creating memories that will linger long after you've left its cobblestone streets behind.

2.6 Local Festivals and Events

Dublin is a city that knows how to celebrate, with its calendar brimming with festivals and events that highlight its vibrant culture and community spirit. These gatherings, often infused with music, art, and traditional Irish charm, offer a unique lens through which to experience the city's dynamic character. From the bustling streets during St. Patrick's Day to the quiet enchantment of a literary festival, Dublin's local events provide an immersive experience for both residents and visitors alike.

One of the most iconic celebrations is the St. Patrick's Festival, held annually in March. This multi-day extravaganza honors Ireland's patron saint with a citywide celebration that attracts visitors from around the globe. The highlight is the St. Patrick's Day Parade, a colorful procession that winds through the heart of Dublin, featuring elaborate floats, marching bands, and performers. The city comes alive with music, dance, and festivities, as locals and tourists alike don green attire to join in the merriment. Beyond the parade, the festival includes cultural events, street performances, and food markets, offering a comprehensive taste of Irish culture and hospitality.

For those with a love of literature, the Dublin Book Festival is a must-attend event celebrating the city's rich literary heritage. Typically held in November, the festival features a diverse program of readings, workshops, and discussions with authors and poets. Set in various venues around the city, such as Smock Alley Theatre and the National Library of Ireland, the festival provides an intimate setting for literary enthusiasts to engage with Irish and international writers. It's an opportunity to delve into the written word and share in the lively exchanges that define Dublin's literary scene.

The Dublin Theatre Festival, another cultural cornerstone, takes place in late September and early October, showcasing the best in Irish and international theater. Established in 1957, it is one of Europe's longest-running theater festivals, offering a platform for both established and emerging artists. Audiences can enjoy a diverse array of performances, from classic plays to innovative contemporary works, staged in venues across the city. The festival fosters creativity and dialogue, inviting theatergoers to experience new perspectives and powerful storytelling.

Food enthusiasts will relish the Taste of Dublin, a gastronomic event held in the picturesque surroundings of the Iveagh Gardens each June. This open-air festival brings together top chefs, restaurants, and food producers to celebrate Dublin's evolving culinary scene. Attendees can sample dishes from some of the city's finest eateries, participate in cooking demonstrations, and discover the latest food trends. It's a vibrant celebration of flavor and creativity, where food lovers can indulge their senses and mingle with like-minded individuals.

Dublin's love for music is evident in the eclectic lineup of events throughout the year, including the Longitude Festival, held annually in Marlay Park. This popular music festival, typically taking place in July, features a mix of international and local acts spanning genres from pop and rock to electronic and hip-hop. With its lively atmosphere and diverse lineup, Longitude is a highlight of Dublin's summer, drawing music lovers to enjoy performances in the park's scenic setting.

For a more traditional experience, the Dublin Tradfest offers a celebration of Irish music and culture every January. Taking place in historic venues such as Dublin Castle and St. Patrick's Cathedral, the festival showcases the best of Irish traditional music, with performances by renowned musicians and emerging talents. Alongside the concerts, the festival features workshops, masterclasses, and family-friendly events, providing an immersive experience in the sounds and rhythms of Ireland's musical heritage.

Art lovers will find inspiration at the Dublin Fringe Festival, a dynamic showcase of new and innovative work across various art forms. Held in September, the festival presents a lineup of theater, dance, visual arts, and more, pushing the boundaries of creative expression. With performances taking place in unconventional spaces around the city, the Fringe Festival encourages audiences to explore Dublin's artistic landscape and engage with bold, thought-provoking work.

The Dublin International Film Festival, held in February, celebrates the art of cinema with a diverse program of screenings, premieres, and panel discussions. Showcasing films from Ireland and around the world, the festival provides a platform for filmmakers to share their stories and connect with audiences. With screenings held in iconic venues such as the Lighthouse Cinema and the Irish Film Institute, the festival offers film enthusiasts an opportunity to experience the magic of cinema in the heart of Dublin.

For those interested in history and culture, the Bloomsday Festival is a unique event that celebrates the life and work of James Joyce, particularly his iconic novel "Ulysses." Held on June 16th, the festival invites participants to dress in Edwardian attire and follow in the footsteps of the novel's protagonist, Leopold Bloom, through the streets of Dublin. The day is filled with readings, performances, and reenactments, offering an engaging way to explore Joyce's literary legacy and Dublin's past.

These festivals and events, each with its own distinct flavor and charm, reflect the diversity and vibrancy of Dublin's cultural scene. They offer an opportunity to connect with the city's artistic, literary, and culinary heritage, while also celebrating its contemporary spirit. Whether you're a resident or a visitor, experiencing Dublin through its local festivals provides a deeper understanding of the city's unique character and the warmth of its community. As you partake in these celebrations, you'll find that Dublin is a city that embraces life with open arms, inviting all to join in its joyful dance.

CHAPTER 3: ANCIENT CASTLES AND RUINS

3.1 The Mystique of Irish Castles

Ireland's landscape, dotted with ancient castles, evokes a sense of mystery and wonder that captivates the imagination. These storied fortresses, each with its own unique tale, stand as silent witnesses to centuries of history, romance, and intrigue. The allure of Irish castles lies not only in their architectural grandeur but also in the legends and folklore that surround them, offering a captivating glimpse into Ireland's past.

Begin your journey with Dublin Castle, a landmark that has played a pivotal role in the city's history since its foundation in the early 13th century. Originally constructed as a defensive fortification, the castle evolved over the centuries into a symbol of British rule in Ireland. Today, it serves as a government complex and cultural venue, with its medieval tower, State Apartments, and Chapel Royal open to visitors. As you explore its hallowed halls, imagine the political machinations and royal ceremonies that once unfolded within its walls, echoing the complex history of Ireland's relationship with the British crown.

A short drive from Dublin lies the imposing Malahide Castle, one of Ireland's oldest and most storied castles. Nestled amidst 260 acres of lush parkland, this castle was home to the Talbot family for nearly 800 years. The castle's interior, adorned with period furnishings and artwork, offers a glimpse into the aristocratic life of its former inhabitants. Legend has it that the castle is haunted by several ghosts, including Puck, a jester who roams its halls, adding an air of mystique to its storied past. Guided tours provide insight into the castle's history and the lives of those who once called it home.

Travel further afield to the iconic Blarney Castle, renowned worldwide for its Blarney Stone. Nestled in the picturesque countryside near Cork, the castle dates back to the 15th century and is steeped in legend. The Blarney Stone, set high in the castle's battlements, is said to bestow the gift of eloquence upon those who kiss it. Visitors must lean backward over a sheer drop to reach the stone, an experience that combines thrill with tradition. Beyond the stone, the castle's gardens, with their winding pathways and mystical features, invite exploration and reflection.

In the heart of County Clare stands Bunratty Castle, a formidable 15th-century fortress that offers a window into medieval Ireland. The castle's meticulously restored interiors and period furnishings recreate the atmosphere of a bygone era, transporting visitors to a time of lords and ladies. Each evening, the castle hosts a medieval banquet, complete with traditional music and entertainment, providing a taste of Ireland's rich cultural heritage. The surrounding Bunratty Folk Park further enhances the experience, with its recreation of a 19th-century Irish village offering insight into rural life of the past.

Ashford Castle, located on the shores of Lough Corrib in County Mayo, exemplifies the opulence and romance of Ireland's castellated heritage. This 13th-century castle has been transformed into a luxury hotel, offering guests a taste of regal living amidst its elegant surroundings. The castle's turrets and towers rise majestically above manicured gardens and woodlands, creating an enchanting backdrop for relaxation and exploration. Guests can partake in a variety of activities, from falconry to boating, immersing themselves in the castle's storied ambiance.

Looming over the landscape of County Offaly is Leap Castle, reputed to be one of Ireland's most haunted castles. Built in the late 15th century, it has a dark and tumultuous history marked by clan rivalries and gruesome events. The castle's eerie reputation is fueled by tales of its resident spirits, including the infamous Elemental, a malevolent presence said to haunt its corridors. Despite—or perhaps because of—its chilling past, Leap Castle attracts those with a fascination for the supernatural and the macabre, offering ghost tours and paranormal investigations for the brave at heart.

Kilkenny Castle, situated along the River Nore in the medieval city of Kilkenny, combines historical significance with architectural beauty. Originally constructed in the 12th century, the castle has undergone extensive restoration, preserving its grandeur for future generations. Visitors can explore the castle's elegant rooms, adorned with artwork and period furnishings, and stroll through its extensive gardens and parklands. Kilkenny Castle also hosts art exhibitions and cultural events, serving as a vibrant hub for the city's artistic community.

A visit to the Rock of Cashel in County Tipperary offers a breathtaking view of medieval ecclesiastical architecture. Perched on a limestone hill, this ancient site is home to a collection of historic buildings, including a round tower, a cathedral, and a chapel adorned with stunning frescoes. The site, traditionally associated with the conversion of the Irish to Christianity, holds immense cultural and spiritual significance. As you wander among its ruins, the panoramic views of the surrounding countryside provide a moment of reflection and awe.

Each castle, with its own unique character and history, adds to the mystique and allure of Ireland's landscape. Whether you are drawn to tales of haunting spirits, the grandeur of aristocratic life, or the thrill of historical exploration, these castles invite you to step back in time and experience the magic of Ireland's storied past. They serve as reminders of the country's complex history, offering a tangible connection to the legends and lore that have shaped its identity.

As you explore these enduring symbols of Ireland's heritage, you uncover stories of bravery, betrayal, romance, and resilience. The castles stand as testaments to the past, inviting you to lose yourself in their enchanting narratives and create your own memories amidst their ancient walls. Through their battlements and banquet halls, Ireland's castles offer a journey through time, where history comes alive and the spirit of the Emerald Isle is felt in every stone.

3.2 Top Castles to Visit

Ireland's landscape, adorned with castles that rise majestically against the horizon, offers a journey into the past where history and legend intertwine. These fortresses, each unique in their architecture and stories, provide a glimpse into the country's rich heritage. For travelers seeking to explore the most captivating of these historic sites, a selection of Ireland's top castles promises an unforgettable adventure through time.

Begin your exploration with Kilkenny Castle, a striking symbol of medieval Ireland situated in the heart of Kilkenny City. Constructed in the 12th century by the powerful Butler family, the castle has withstood centuries of change, evolving from a defensive stronghold to a stately home. Today, its meticulously restored interiors offer a window into the opulent lifestyle of its former inhabitants. Visitors can wander through grand rooms adorned with tapestries and portraits, while the extensive parklands provide a serene setting for a leisurely stroll.

Journey north to the imposing Dunluce Castle, perched dramatically on the cliffs of County Antrim. This 16th-century ruin boasts breathtaking views of the North Atlantic and is steeped in tales of intrigue and mystery. Legend has it that part of the castle's kitchen collapsed into the sea during a storm, adding to its reputation as one of Ireland's most haunted sites. As you explore the remnants of its stone walls and towers, the castle's history as a seat of the MacDonnell clan comes alive, offering a hauntingly beautiful experience.

In the west of Ireland, the magnificent Ashford Castle captivates with its fairy-tale charm and luxurious accommodations. Originally built in the 13th century, this castle has been transformed into a five-star hotel, welcoming guests to indulge in its regal splendor. The sprawling estate, nestled on the shores of Lough Corrib, offers a plethora of activities, from falconry and horseback riding to golf and spa treatments. Whether you're staying overnight or visiting for the day, Ashford Castle promises an enchanting experience amidst its turrets and towers.

Travel to the south to discover the historic Blarney Castle, home to the famous Blarney Stone. Visitors from around the world flock to this 15th-century stronghold to kiss the stone, said to bestow the gift of eloquence upon those who dare. The castle's lush gardens invite exploration, with their meandering paths leading to mystical features such as the Poison Garden and the Witch's Stone. Beyond the legend, Blarney Castle offers a captivating glimpse into Ireland's medieval past, where history and folklore merge.

For a truly unique experience, visit Rock of Cashel, a dramatic complex of medieval buildings perched atop a limestone hill in County Tipperary. Once the seat of the Kings of Munster, this historic site boasts an impressive collection of religious and royal architecture, including a round tower, a cathedral, and the stunning Cormac's Chapel. The panoramic views from the hilltop are breathtaking, providing a perfect backdrop for contemplation and appreciation of Ireland's rich cultural heritage.

Venture to the rugged landscapes of County Clare to discover Bunratty Castle, a beautifully preserved 15th-century fortress that offers a window into the past. The castle's interior, furnished with authentic medieval artifacts, transports visitors to a time of knights and chieftains. Each evening, Bunratty Castle hosts a medieval banquet, complete with traditional music and entertainment, allowing guests to immerse themselves in the spirit of the era. The adjacent folk park further enriches the experience, recreating 19th-century rural life with its charming village and working farm.

Explore the enchanting Kylemore Abbey, set against the backdrop of Connemara's stunning mountains and lakes. Originally built as a private residence in the 19th century, the abbey is now home to a community of Benedictine nuns. Visitors can tour the opulent Victorian rooms, stroll through the beautifully restored walled gardens, and reflect in the tranquility of the neo-Gothic church. Kylemore Abbey offers a serene and spiritual retreat, where history, art, and nature harmoniously converge.

In the heart of County Limerick, the formidable King John's Castle stands proudly on the banks of the River Shannon. Built in the early 13th century, the castle has played a pivotal role in Irish history, witnessing sieges, battles, and political intrigue. Today, its interactive exhibitions and medieval courtyard bring the past to life, providing a fascinating insight into the castle's storied past. Climb the battlements for panoramic views of Limerick City and beyond, capturing the essence of a bygone era.

For those intrigued by tales of the supernatural, Leap Castle in County Offaly is a must-visit. Often cited as one of Ireland's most haunted castles, its history is shrouded in mystery and legend. The castle has been home to numerous clans and families, each leaving their mark on its turbulent past. Visitors can explore its atmospheric rooms and learn about the castle's ghostly residents, including the infamous Elemental. Leap Castle offers a spine-chilling journey into the unknown, where history and hauntings intertwine.

Conclude your castle tour with a visit to the majestic Cahir Castle, one of Ireland's largest and best-preserved castles. Situated on an island in the River Suir, this 13th-century fortress boasts an impressive array of defensive features, including a drawbridge, towers, and battlements. The castle's history is brought to life through guided tours and multimedia exhibits, offering a comprehensive exploration of its architectural and historical significance. Cahir Castle stands as a testament to Ireland's medieval heritage, inviting visitors to step back in time and experience the grandeur of its storied past.

These top castles, each with its own unique charm and history, offer a journey through Ireland's rich and varied past. From the haunting ruins of Dunluce Castle to the luxurious elegance of Ashford Castle, these historic sites invite exploration and discovery. As you wander through their halls and grounds, you'll uncover the stories and legends that have shaped Ireland's cultural landscape, creating memories that will linger long after your visit. Whether you're drawn to tales of romance, intrigue, or the supernatural, Ireland's castles promise an adventure that captures the imagination and the heart.

3.3 Ruins with a Story

Ireland's landscape is a tapestry of ancient ruins, each whispering stories of the past through their weathered stones and crumbling walls. These sites, steeped in history and legend, offer a unique opportunity to connect with the souls of bygone eras. As you wander through these hauntingly beautiful remnants, you'll find yourself transported to a time when these ruins were vibrant centers of life, power, and spirituality.

One of the most evocative ruins is the monastic settlement of Glendalough, nestled in the verdant Wicklow Mountains. Founded in the 6th century by St. Kevin, this site once thrived as a hub of religious devotion and learning. Today, visitors can explore the remains of its stone churches, round tower, and ancient graveyard. As you walk the serene paths along the glacial lakes, the echoes of monks chanting in long-forgotten prayers seem to linger in the air. Glendalough invites contemplation, offering a glimpse into the monastic life that once flourished here.

Another remarkable site is the Rock of Dunamase, a fortress that stands atop a hill in County Laois, commanding panoramic views of the surrounding countryside. This ancient stronghold dates back to the early medieval period and has witnessed a tumultuous history of battles and sieges. As you explore the remnants of its curtain walls and gatehouse, imagine the fierce warriors who once defended this strategic location. The Rock of Dunamase, with its rugged beauty and storied past, offers a powerful connection to Ireland's martial heritage.

In the heart of the Burren in County Clare lies the ancient Poulnabrone Dolmen, a portal tomb that dates back to the Neolithic period. This iconic structure, with its massive capstone balanced atop slender uprights, stands as a testament to the ingenuity and spiritual beliefs of Ireland's early inhabitants. Archaeological excavations have uncovered human remains and artifacts, offering insights into the rituals and customs of those who lived over 5,000 years ago. As you stand before this enigmatic monument, the mysteries of Ireland's prehistoric past unfold before you.

The haunting ruins of the medieval town of Clonmacnoise, located on the banks of the River Shannon in County Offaly, tell the story of a once-thriving monastic community. Founded in the 6th century, Clonmacnoise became a center of religion, trade, and craftsmanship, attracting scholars and pilgrims from across Europe. Today, the site is home to the remains of churches, a round tower, and intricately carved high crosses. As you explore this atmospheric site, the spirit of the monks who dedicated their lives to learning and devotion seems to linger, inviting reflection on Ireland's spiritual legacy.

On the windswept Aran Islands, the ancient fort of Dun Aonghasa clings to the edge of a sheer cliff, offering breathtaking views of the Atlantic Ocean. This prehistoric stone fort, with its concentric walls and defensive features, dates back to the Iron Age. As you walk along the cliff's edge, the sheer drop to the sea below serves as a reminder of the fort's strategic significance. The raw beauty and isolation of Dun Aonghasa evoke a sense of awe and wonder, connecting you to the ancient peoples who once called this rugged landscape home.

In County Meath, the Hill of Tara stands as a symbol of Ireland's ancient royal heritage. This historic site, once the seat of the High Kings of Ireland, is steeped in mythology and folklore. Among the ruins are the Mound of the Hostages, an ancient burial site, and the Lia Fáil, or Stone of Destiny, said to roar when touched by the rightful king. As you walk the grassy mounds and earthworks, the legends of Tara come alive, weaving a tapestry of myth and history that has shaped Ireland's cultural identity.

A journey to the west brings you to the hauntingly beautiful ruins of Aughnanure Castle in County Galway. Nestled by the banks of the River Drimneen, this 16th-century tower house was once the stronghold of the O'Flaherty clan. The castle's strategic location and formidable design speak to the turbulent times in which it was built. As you explore the remnants of its banquet hall and battlements, the stories of clan rivalries and power struggles echo through its stone walls, painting a vivid picture of Ireland's feudal past.

The ancient stone circles of Drombeg in County Cork offer a captivating glimpse into Ireland's prehistoric past. This well-preserved circle, consisting of seventeen standing stones, served as a ceremonial site for early inhabitants. Archaeological evidence suggests that rituals and gatherings took place here, reflecting the spiritual beliefs and social structures of the time. As you stand within the circle, the alignment of the stones with the setting sun during the winter solstice invites reflection on the harmony between nature and human existence.

The ruins of Sligo Abbey, a Dominican friary founded in the 13th century, provide insight into Ireland's medieval ecclesiastical architecture. Despite the ravages of time, the abbey's cloisters, lancet windows, and intricately carved tombs remain, offering a glimpse into the monastic life that once thrived within its walls. As you wander through the atmospheric ruins, the echoes of prayers and chants seem to resonate, connecting you to a time when the abbey was a vibrant center of spirituality and learning.

Finally, the poignant ruins of Jerpoint Abbey in County Kilkenny offer a testament to the architectural and artistic achievements of Ireland's Cistercian monks. Founded in the 12th century, the abbey boasts stunning stone carvings and a beautifully preserved cloister arcade. As you explore the site, the stories of the monks who lived and worked here come to life, illustrating their devotion to faith and craftsmanship.

These ruins, each with their own unique stories and significance, provide a window into Ireland's rich tapestry of history and culture. As you explore these ancient sites, you'll uncover the stories of the people who once lived, worshiped, and fought within their walls. The allure of these ruins lies not only in their architectural beauty but in the tales they tell, inviting you to embark on a journey through time and connect with the soul of Ireland's past.

3.4 Guided Tours vs. Solo Exploration

When it comes to experiencing the rich tapestry of Ireland's historical sites and breathtaking landscapes, travelers often face the decision between joining a guided tour or embarking on a solo exploration. Each approach offers its own set of advantages and challenges, catering to different preferences and travel styles. Understanding the nuances of both options can help you make the most of your Irish adventure.

Guided tours provide the convenience of structured itineraries and expert insights, often led by knowledgeable guides who bring the history and culture of Ireland to life. These tours can range from intimate groups to larger, more comprehensive excursions, each offering a curated experience that highlights the must-see landmarks and hidden gems. One of the key benefits of guided tours is the ease of logistics. Transportation, accommodations, and entry fees are typically arranged in advance, allowing travelers to focus on enjoying the journey without the stress of planning. Additionally, guides often share captivating stories and historical context, enriching the experience with anecdotes and local lore that might otherwise be missed.

For those who value social interaction, guided tours offer the opportunity to connect with fellow travelers from around the world. The shared experiences and camaraderie that develop within a group setting can enhance the enjoyment of exploring Ireland's cultural and natural wonders. Whether it's a lively discussion over dinner or bonding during a scenic hike, the sense of community can add a memorable dimension to the trip.

However, guided tours may come with certain limitations. The structured nature of these tours means that itineraries are often predetermined, leaving little room for spontaneity or personal exploration. Travelers who prefer to linger at a particular site or venture off the beaten path might find the rigid schedule restricting. Additionally, the experience of traveling in a group may not suit those who prefer solitude or a more personalized journey.

On the other hand, solo exploration offers the freedom to tailor your travels to your own interests and pace. Ireland's well-connected transportation network and welcoming hospitality make it an ideal destination for independent travelers. With the ability to choose your own path, you can immerse yourself in the experiences that resonate most with you, whether it's wandering through a quaint village, hiking along the rugged coastline, or delving into the vibrant arts scene of a bustling city.

The flexibility of solo travel allows you to adapt your itinerary based on weather, mood, or newfound discoveries. If you stumble upon a charming café or a local festival, you have the freedom to pause and savor the moment. This spontaneity can lead to unexpected adventures and encounters, enriching your journey with unique stories and memories.

Solo exploration also encourages a deeper connection with the environment and culture. Without the influence of a group, you may engage more closely with locals, seeking recommendations and insights that offer an authentic perspective on Irish life. These interactions can provide valuable context and enrich your understanding of the places you visit.

However, independent travel requires a level of self-reliance and preparation. Navigating unfamiliar terrain, organizing accommodations, and managing logistics can be challenging, particularly for first-time visitors. It's important to conduct thorough research and plan ahead to ensure a smooth and enjoyable experience. Additionally, traveling alone may sometimes lead to feelings of isolation, especially in remote areas or during moments of cultural unfamiliarity.

Ultimately, the choice between guided tours and solo exploration depends on personal preferences and travel goals. For those who value convenience, expert guidance, and social interaction, guided tours offer a structured and informative way to experience Ireland. Conversely, travelers who seek flexibility, independence, and a personalized journey may find solo exploration more fulfilling.

For a balanced approach, consider combining elements of both options. Joining a guided tour for specific regions or activities can provide insight and ease, while allocating time for independent exploration allows for personal discovery and spontaneity. This hybrid approach enables you to enjoy the best of both worlds, tailoring your journey to suit your interests and preferences.

Whichever path you choose, Ireland's enchanting landscapes and rich cultural heritage promise a rewarding and unforgettable experience. Whether guided by the stories of a seasoned tour leader or the whispers of ancient ruins discovered on your own, the journey through Ireland is bound to leave an indelible mark on your heart and mind. As you explore the Emerald Isle, embrace the spirit of adventure and curiosity, allowing the journey to unfold in ways both planned and unexpected.

3.5 Photography Tips for Castles

Capturing the mystique and grandeur of castles through photography can be an immensely rewarding endeavor. These architectural marvels, with their imposing facades and intricate details, provide endless opportunities for stunning and evocative images. Whether you are a seasoned photographer or a beginner, understanding some key techniques and tips can help you create compelling castle photographs that convey the essence of these historic structures.

The first step in photographing castles is to plan your visit strategically. Lighting plays a crucial role in photography, and castles are no exception. The golden hours—shortly after sunrise and just before sunset—offer soft, warm light that can enhance the textures and colors of the stonework, creating a captivating atmosphere. During these times, shadows are longer and more pronounced, adding depth and dimension to your images. If possible, schedule your visit to coincide with these ideal lighting conditions to make the most of your photography session.

When approaching a castle, take time to explore different vantage points and angles. Often, the most striking images are those that capture the castle in a way that highlights its unique features. Consider shooting from a low angle to emphasize the height and grandeur of the towers, or find a high vantage point to capture the castle in its entirety within the landscape. Pay attention to the surroundings—whether it's a moat, a garden, or a dramatic sky—and use them to frame your composition and add context to your photograph.

Incorporating foreground elements can also enhance your castle photography. Look for natural elements like trees, flowers, or archways that can serve as a frame or lead the viewer's eye into the scene. These elements can provide a sense of scale and depth, making the castle appear more majestic and three-dimensional.

Another technique to consider is the use of reflections. If the castle is situated near a body of water, such as a lake or river, take advantage of the reflective surface to create a mirrored image of the structure. This can result in a visually striking composition, where the reflection adds symmetry and intrigue to your photograph.

Detail shots are equally important in capturing the essence of a castle. Zoom in on architectural features such as ornate doorways, intricate carvings, or weathered stone walls to highlight the craftsmanship and character of the structure. These close-up shots can tell a different part of the castle's story, focusing on the elements that might be overlooked in wider compositions.

When photographing the interior of a castle, be mindful of the lighting conditions, which can vary greatly. Interiors often have limited natural light, so adjusting your camera settings is crucial. Consider using a higher ISO setting to compensate for low light, but be cautious of introducing too much noise into your image. A tripod can be invaluable in such situations, allowing you to use slower shutter speeds without sacrificing sharpness.

Composition is key when capturing the grandeur of castle interiors. Look for leading lines, such as corridors or staircases, that draw the viewer's eye through the frame. Symmetry can also be a powerful compositional tool, especially in rooms with grand architecture or opulent decorations. Experiment with different perspectives to find the composition that best conveys the atmosphere of the space.

Post-processing can further enhance your castle photographs, bringing out details and colors that might not be immediately apparent. Adjusting the contrast and saturation can add vibrancy and drama to your images, while careful cropping can improve composition and focus attention on key elements. However, strive to maintain the authenticity of the scene, ensuring that your edits complement rather than overshadow the natural beauty of the castle.

For those who wish to delve deeper into castle photography, consider experimenting with different techniques such as long exposures or black-and-white photography. Long exposures can create ethereal effects, such as blurring moving clouds or capturing the smooth surface of water, adding a dreamlike quality to your images. Black-and-white photography, on the other hand, can emphasize textures and contrasts, stripping away color to focus on the form and structure of the castle.

Finally, remember that every castle has its own unique story and character. As you photograph these historic sites, consider the narrative you wish to convey through your images. Whether it's the imposing presence of a medieval fortress, the romantic allure of a fairy-tale castle, or the haunting beauty of a ruin, let your photographs reflect the emotions and impressions that the castle evokes in you.

In conclusion, capturing the beauty and grandeur of castles through photography requires a blend of technical skills and creative vision. By planning your visit, experimenting with different techniques, and paying attention to composition and lighting, you can create images that not only document the architectural splendor of these structures but also convey their timeless magic and allure. As you explore and photograph these historic sites, let your creativity and passion guide you, allowing your images to tell the story of each castle in your own unique way.

3.6 Preservation and History

The preservation of historical sites is a delicate dance between safeguarding the past and accommodating the needs of the present. Castles, with their imposing stone walls and storied pasts, stand as testaments to the architectural ingenuity and cultural significance of bygone eras. These structures, scattered across the landscape, serve as vital links to history, offering insights into the lives, conflicts, and aspirations of those who once inhabited them. The task of preserving these monuments requires a nuanced understanding of both their historical context and the challenges posed by modern conservation efforts.

Preserving a castle involves more than merely maintaining its physical structure; it requires a commitment to understanding its historical significance and the stories embedded within its walls. Each castle carries with it a unique narrative, shaped by the political, social, and economic forces of its time. To truly appreciate these ancient edifices, one must delve into the historical context that gave rise to their construction. Many castles were built as defensive fortresses, strategically positioned to protect against invasions or uprisings. Others served as symbols of power and prestige, showcasing the wealth and influence of their owners.

The preservation process begins with a thorough assessment of the castle's current condition. This involves detailed surveys and inspections to identify any structural weaknesses, weathering, or damage caused by time and the elements. Conservationists work diligently to stabilize these structures, employing techniques that range from traditional craftsmanship to cutting-edge technology. The goal is to preserve as much of the original material as possible while ensuring the castle's safety and longevity.

One of the primary challenges in castle preservation is balancing the need for structural integrity with the desire to maintain historical authenticity. Modern interventions must be carefully planned and executed to respect the original design and materials. This often involves working with skilled artisans who specialize in traditional building techniques, such as stonemasonry and lime mortar application. These craftsmen play a crucial role in restoring damaged sections of the castle, using methods that would have been familiar to the original builders.

In addition to physical restoration, preserving the history of a castle involves meticulous documentation and research. Archivists and historians examine historical records, maps, and other sources to piece together the stories of the people who lived and worked within these walls. This research helps to inform conservation efforts, ensuring that restoration work aligns with the castle's historical context and significance. By understanding the castle's past, preservationists can make informed decisions about how best to protect its legacy for future generations.

Public engagement is another vital aspect of castle preservation. By opening these sites to visitors, preservationists can share the rich history and cultural significance of castles with a wider audience. Educational programs, guided tours, and interpretive displays provide opportunities for visitors to connect with the past, fostering a deeper appreciation for the historical and architectural heritage of these structures. This engagement not only raises awareness of the importance of preservation but also generates support for ongoing conservation efforts.

The preservation of castles also involves addressing the environmental and economic factors that can impact their longevity. Climate change poses a significant threat to these historic sites, with rising temperatures and increased rainfall accelerating the deterioration of stone and mortar. Conservationists must adapt their strategies to mitigate these effects, exploring new materials and techniques that can withstand the changing environment while remaining true to the castle's original construction.

Economic pressures also play a role in preservation efforts. The costs associated with maintaining and restoring castles can be substantial, requiring funding from both public and private sources. Many castles have embraced innovative approaches to sustainability, such as hosting events or offering accommodation, to generate revenue that supports their upkeep. These initiatives not only provide financial stability but also create new opportunities for people to experience and appreciate these historic sites.

International collaboration is essential in the field of castle preservation. By sharing knowledge, expertise, and resources, conservationists can learn from each other's successes and challenges, advancing the field as a whole. Global organizations and networks dedicated to heritage preservation play a crucial role in facilitating these exchanges, promoting best practices and encouraging cross-cultural understanding.

Ultimately, the preservation of castles is a testament to our collective commitment to safeguarding our shared cultural heritage. These structures, with their enduring beauty and historical significance, serve as reminders of the complex and often tumultuous history that has shaped our world. By preserving and honoring these monuments, we ensure that future generations can continue to learn from and be inspired by the stories of the past.

In preserving castles, we do more than protect stone and mortar; we preserve the legacy of those who came before us, ensuring that their stories continue to resonate through the ages. As we walk through the halls and courtyards of these ancient structures, we are reminded of the resilience and creativity of the human spirit, and the enduring power of history to connect us across time and space.

CHAPTER 4: SCENIC DRIVES AND NATURAL WONDERS

4.1 The Wild Atlantic Way

Stretching over 1,500 miles along Ireland's rugged west coast, the Wild Atlantic Way is a spectacular driving route that showcases the untamed beauty and rich cultural heritage of the Emerald Isle. This iconic journey takes travelers through nine counties, from the Inishowen Peninsula in County Donegal to Kinsale in County Cork, weaving along cliffs, beaches, and picturesque villages. Each bend in the road reveals awe-inspiring vistas and hidden treasures, inviting explorers to delve into Ireland's natural splendor and vibrant local traditions.

The journey begins in the dramatic landscapes of County Donegal, where the Slieve League Cliffs offer some of the highest sea cliffs in Europe. These towering cliffs provide a breathtaking introduction to the Wild Atlantic Way, with views that stretch across the Atlantic Ocean. The area is steeped in history and folklore, with ancient ruins and megalithic tombs dotting the landscape. From here, the route meanders through the scenic beauty of County Sligo, where the majestic Benbulben Mountain stands sentinel over Yeats Country. This region, immortalized in the poetry of W.B. Yeats, captivates with its mystical landscapes and rich literary heritage.

Continuing south, the Wild Atlantic Way leads to the enchanting landscapes of County Mayo, home to the iconic Croagh Patrick. This sacred mountain, a site of pilgrimage for centuries, offers climbers panoramic views of Clew Bay and its countless islands. Mayo's rugged coastline is dotted with charming villages, such as Westport, where travelers can experience the warmth of Irish hospitality and indulge in local cuisine.

As the journey unfolds, the route enters the strikingly beautiful region of Connemara in County Galway. Known for its wild, windswept landscapes, Connemara captivates with its bogs, mountains, and pristine beaches. The area is a haven for outdoor enthusiasts, offering opportunities for hiking, cycling, and fishing. The vibrant city of Galway, with its lively arts scene and traditional music, provides a cultural counterpoint to Connemara's natural beauty. Strolling through Galway's cobbled streets, visitors can experience the city's unique blend of history and modernity.

Further south, the Wild Atlantic Way leads to the dramatic Cliffs of Moher in County Clare. These iconic cliffs, rising over 700 feet above the Atlantic, offer breathtaking views that attract visitors from around the world. The rugged Burren region, with its unique limestone landscape and rich biodiversity, provides a stark contrast to the cliffs' sheer beauty. This area is home to ancient archaeological sites and traditional Irish music, offering a glimpse into Ireland's cultural and natural heritage.

As the route continues into County Kerry, travelers encounter the stunning Ring of Kerry. This scenic drive takes in sweeping coastal views, lush green landscapes, and charming towns such as Killarney and Kenmare. The dramatic beauty of the Iveragh Peninsula, with its mountains and lakes, offers endless opportunities for outdoor adventures, from hiking and cycling to kayaking and golfing. Here, the Wild Atlantic Way reveals the essence of Ireland's untamed spirit, with landscapes that inspire awe and wonder.

The journey through County Cork brings travelers to the picturesque Beara Peninsula, a region of rugged beauty and rich history. The peninsula's narrow, winding roads lead to hidden coves and ancient stone circles, offering a sense of discovery and adventure. The vibrant town of Kinsale, known for its colorful streets and gourmet cuisine, provides a fitting conclusion to the Wild Atlantic Way. Here, travelers can savor the flavors of the sea and reflect on the journey's many wonders.

Throughout the Wild Atlantic Way, the rhythm of the ocean provides a constant backdrop, shaping the landscapes and the lives of those who call this region home. The route is not just a journey through breathtaking scenery; it is an exploration of Ireland's cultural tapestry, woven with stories of resilience, creativity, and community. Each village and town along the way offers a unique perspective on Ireland's heritage, from traditional crafts and music to contemporary art and cuisine.

The Wild Atlantic Way also invites travelers to engage with the natural world in meaningful ways. Birdwatching along the cliffs, kayaking in sheltered bays, and hiking across windswept moors offer opportunities to connect with Ireland's diverse ecosystems. Conservation efforts throughout the region aim to protect these landscapes for future generations, ensuring that the Wild Atlantic Way remains a sanctuary for wildlife and a haven for those seeking solace in nature.

As travelers journey along the Wild Atlantic Way, they are encouraged to slow down and savor the experience. The route offers countless opportunities for reflection and connection, whether through quiet moments on a deserted beach or lively conversations in a local pub. The spirit of the Wild Atlantic Way lies in its ability to inspire a sense of wonder and discovery, inviting those who traverse its path to create their own stories and memories.

In essence, the Wild Atlantic Way is more than a route; it is an invitation to explore the heart and soul of Ireland. It offers a journey through landscapes that have inspired poets, artists, and dreamers for centuries, revealing a land of untamed beauty and timeless allure. As travelers embark on this epic adventure, they are reminded of the power of nature and the enduring spirit of the people who call this remarkable place home.

4.2 The Ring of Kerry

The Ring of Kerry is a captivating circular route that offers an unforgettable journey through some of Ireland's most stunning landscapes. Spanning approximately 111 miles, this iconic drive is nestled in County Kerry, on the Iveragh Peninsula. Known for its breathtaking vistas, charming towns, and rich historical sites, the Ring of Kerry encapsulates the essence of Ireland's natural beauty and cultural heritage. As you embark on this journey, you'll find yourself immersed in a landscape that is as varied as it is beautiful, with each turn revealing new wonders.

Starting in Killarney, a vibrant town known for its stunning national park, the journey begins with a sense of anticipation. Killarney National Park, with its lush forests, serene lakes, and majestic mountains, is a haven for nature lovers. Here, you can explore the iconic Muckross House and Gardens, a 19th-century mansion set against the backdrop of the stunning Lakes of Killarney. The park's diverse landscapes offer opportunities for hiking, cycling, and horse-drawn carriage tours, allowing you to fully appreciate the area's natural beauty.

As you leave Killarney and head west, the road winds through the picturesque village of Killorglin, famous for its annual Puck Fair, one of Ireland's oldest festivals. This lively event, held each August, celebrates the crowning of a wild goat as king, drawing visitors with its unique blend of tradition and revelry. The charm of Killorglin lies in its warm hospitality and vibrant community spirit, offering a taste of authentic Irish culture.

Continuing along the route, the Ring of Kerry leads to the stunning coastal scenery of Glenbeigh and Rossbeigh Beach. The expansive sands and crashing waves of Rossbeigh Beach provide an idyllic setting for a leisurely walk or a refreshing dip in the Atlantic Ocean. The surrounding hills offer panoramic views of the Dingle Peninsula and the distant Blasket Islands, creating a breathtaking vista that captures the wild beauty of Ireland's western coast.

The journey then takes you through the picturesque village of Cahersiveen, where the ruins of Ballycarbery Castle stand as a testament to the area's rich history. Nearby, the ancient stone forts of Cahergall and Leacanabuaile offer a glimpse into Ireland's early past, with their impressive stone walls and panoramic views of the surrounding countryside. These historic sites invite exploration, evoking a sense of wonder and connection to the island's ancient heritage.

As you approach the town of Waterville, you'll discover a place beloved by Charlie Chaplin, who often vacationed here with his family. The town honors his memory with a statue and an annual film festival, celebrating its connection to the legendary comedian. Waterville's scenic location between Lough Currane and the Atlantic Ocean makes it a popular destination for fishing, golfing, and enjoying the natural beauty of the area.

The route continues to the charming village of Sneem, known for its colorful houses and friendly atmosphere. Sneem is a delightful spot to pause and enjoy a leisurely meal in one of its welcoming pubs or cafes. The village's idyllic setting, nestled between mountains and sea, offers numerous walking trails that allow you to explore the surrounding landscapes and immerse yourself in the tranquility of the area.

As you travel towards Kenmare, the road reveals some of the most dramatic scenery on the Ring of Kerry. The Moll's Gap and Ladies View offer breathtaking panoramas of the Killarney National Park and the MacGillycuddy's Reeks, Ireland's highest mountain range. These vantage points provide perfect opportunities for photography, capturing the grandeur and majesty of the Irish landscape.

Kenmare, a charming town known for its vibrant arts scene and culinary delights, marks the final leg of the journey. The town's lively atmosphere and rich history make it a fitting conclusion to the Ring of Kerry. Here, you can explore the Kenmare Stone Circle, one of the largest in the southwest of Ireland, and delve into the town's history through its many galleries and craft shops.

Throughout the journey, the Ring of Kerry offers countless opportunities to connect with Ireland's natural and cultural heritage. From the ancient stone forts and castles to the vibrant towns and villages, each stop along the way tells a story of the people and landscapes that have shaped this remarkable region. The route's diverse attractions invite exploration and discovery, providing a rich tapestry of experiences that capture the heart and soul of Ireland.

Traveling the Ring of Kerry is not just about the destinations; it's about the journey itself. The winding roads and ever-changing scenery offer a sense of adventure and wonder, inviting you to slow down and savor the experience. Whether you're exploring hidden coves, hiking through lush forests, or simply enjoying a quiet moment by the sea, the Ring of Kerry provides a journey of discovery that stays with you long after you've returned home.

In essence, the Ring of Kerry is a celebration of Ireland's natural beauty and cultural richness. It offers a journey through landscapes that inspire awe and wonder, revealing the enduring spirit and charm of the Emerald Isle. As you embark on this unforgettable adventure, you'll find yourself captivated by the magic of the Ring of Kerry, creating memories and stories that will last a lifetime.

4.3 Coastal Drives and Hidden Beaches

Coastal drives and hidden beaches offer a captivating way to explore the natural beauty and serene landscapes of Ireland. The country's coastline, with its rugged cliffs and pristine sands, beckons travelers to embark on a journey of discovery. These routes lead to secluded coves and unspoiled beaches, where the rhythm of the waves and the call of seabirds create a symphony of tranquility. Along the way, the coastal roads reveal a tapestry of breathtaking vistas, charming villages, and opportunities for adventure that capture the essence of Ireland's maritime allure.

Embarking on a coastal drive is an invitation to experience Ireland's diverse seascapes at your own pace. One such route is the Copper Coast, a UNESCO Global Geopark located in County Waterford. Named for its historical copper mines, this stretch of coastline offers dramatic cliffs, sea stacks, and hidden coves waiting to be explored. Driving along the winding roads, you'll encounter quaint villages like Bunmahon and Stradbally, where you can pause to enjoy a leisurely meal or delve into the area's rich geological history.

Further west, the stunning coastline of County Clare offers a journey through the Burren and the Cliffs of Moher. While the Cliffs of Moher are a well-known tourist destination, the surrounding area is dotted with lesser-known beaches that provide a more secluded experience. Fanore Beach, with its golden sands and panoramic views of the Atlantic, invites visitors to bask in the peace and beauty of its natural surroundings. The nearby Burren National Park offers a stark contrast to the coastal scenery, with its unique limestone landscape and rich biodiversity.

The coastal drive around the Dingle Peninsula in County Kerry is another must-see route. This loop takes you through some of Ireland's most picturesque landscapes, with views of the Blasket Islands and Mount Brandon. Along the way, you'll discover hidden beaches such as Coumeenoole Beach, a secluded cove with turquoise waters and dramatic cliffs. The village of Dingle itself offers a vibrant blend of traditional Irish culture and contemporary art, making it an ideal stop for those seeking both adventure and relaxation.

For those willing to venture off the beaten path, the Ring of Beara in County Cork offers a lesser-known alternative to the more famous Ring of Kerry. This route boasts stunning coastal views and hidden beaches, such as Garnish Beach, a secluded spot with crystal-clear waters and unspoiled sands. The Beara Peninsula is known for its rugged beauty and rich history, with ancient stone circles and standing stones scattered throughout the landscape. As you explore this remote corner of Ireland, you'll find yourself immersed in a world of natural wonder and timeless charm.

The Wild Atlantic Way, one of the world's longest defined coastal routes, offers countless opportunities to discover hidden beaches and secluded coves. Stretching from County Donegal to County Cork, this route encompasses a diverse array of landscapes, from the dramatic cliffs of Slieve League to the tranquil bays of Connemara. Along the way, you'll find hidden gems such as Silver Strand Beach in County Mayo, a pristine stretch of sand surrounded by rolling hills and azure waters. This secluded spot offers a sense of serenity and escape, inviting visitors to unwind and connect with the natural world.

Embarking on a coastal drive also presents opportunities for outdoor adventures and activities. Surfing enthusiasts will find world-class waves along the west coast, with beaches such as Lahinch and Strandhill offering excellent conditions for both beginners and seasoned surfers. For those who prefer a more leisurely pace, coastal walks and hiking trails provide a chance to explore the cliffs, dunes, and headlands on foot. The Kerry Way and the Sheep's Head Way are just two of the many trails that offer breathtaking views and a chance to immerse yourself in the beauty of Ireland's coastal landscapes.

As you traverse these coastal routes, take the time to engage with the local communities and savor the flavors of the sea. Fresh seafood is a highlight of any coastal journey, with local restaurants and pubs offering dishes that showcase the bounty of the Atlantic. Whether it's a plate of freshly caught fish and chips or a bowl of creamy chowder, the culinary delights of Ireland's coast are sure to satisfy the appetite of any traveler.

In addition to the natural beauty and outdoor activities, Ireland's coastal drives offer a glimpse into the country's rich maritime history and cultural heritage. From ancient forts and castles to traditional fishing villages, the coastline is steeped in stories of the past. The village of Cobh in County Cork, for example, is known for its role as the last port of call for the Titanic and offers a poignant reminder of Ireland's connection to the sea. Exploring these historical sites adds depth and context to your journey, enriching your understanding of the people and places that have shaped Ireland's coastal identity.

Ultimately, coastal drives and hidden beaches provide a unique and rewarding way to experience the magic of Ireland's coast. Whether you're seeking adventure, relaxation, or a deeper connection to the land and its history, these routes offer something for everyone. As you wind your way along the coastal roads, let the beauty of the landscape and the rhythm of the ocean guide you to new discoveries and cherished memories. The allure of Ireland's coast lies not only in its breathtaking scenery but also in the sense of freedom and exploration it inspires, inviting you to lose yourself in the wonder of the journey.

4.4 Hiking Trails and Outdoor Adventures

Ireland's hiking trails and outdoor adventures offer a unique way to experience the country's breathtaking landscapes and rich natural heritage. From rugged mountains and lush forests to serene lakes and dramatic coastlines, the diversity of Ireland's terrain provides a wealth of opportunities for exploration and discovery. Whether you're an experienced hiker seeking a challenging ascent or a casual walker looking for a leisurely stroll, the trails and outdoor activities available across the country cater to all levels of experience and ambition.

One of the most iconic hiking destinations in Ireland is the Wicklow Mountains National Park, located just south of Dublin. This vast expanse of wilderness encompasses a range of landscapes, from rolling hills and deep glacial valleys to picturesque lakes and dense woodlands. The park offers a variety of trails, each with its own unique character and challenges. The Wicklow Way, Ireland's oldest long-distance walking route, stretches for over 80 miles and provides a comprehensive tour of the region's natural beauty. As you traverse this trail, you'll encounter historic sites, such as the ancient monastic settlement of Glendalough, nestled within the lush valley surrounded by towering cliffs.

For those seeking a more challenging adventure, the ascent of Croagh Patrick in County Mayo offers both a physical test and a spiritual journey. Known as Ireland's holiest mountain, Croagh Patrick has been a site of pilgrimage for centuries, with thousands of people climbing its steep slopes each year, especially on Reek Sunday. The climb to the summit is steep and demanding, but the panoramic views of Clew Bay and the surrounding countryside make the effort worthwhile. At the peak, a small chapel stands as a testament to the mountain's religious significance.

In the southwest, the rugged beauty of the Beara Peninsula provides a haven for outdoor enthusiasts. The Beara Way, a long-distance walking trail, encircles the peninsula, offering stunning coastal views and encounters with local wildlife. This trail is less traveled than others, providing a sense of solitude and tranquility as you explore its hidden gems. The route passes through charming villages, ancient stone circles, and dramatic landscapes, allowing hikers to immerse themselves in the unique character of this remote region.

The Connemara National Park in County Galway is another must-visit destination for those who love the outdoors. This park's diverse landscapes include mountains, bogs, grasslands, and woodlands, providing a rich tapestry of habitats to explore. The Diamond Hill Loop is a popular trail that offers a moderate climb with rewarding views of the Twelve Bens mountain range and the Atlantic Ocean. Connemara's wild and untamed beauty captivates all who visit, with its ever-changing skies and vibrant colors.

For a coastal adventure, the Cliffs of Moher Coastal Walk in County Clare provides a thrilling experience along one of Ireland's most dramatic natural features. This trail runs along the edge of the cliffs, offering breathtaking views of the Atlantic Ocean and the Aran Islands. The path is well-marked but requires caution, as the cliffs drop sharply to the sea below. Walking this trail allows you to fully appreciate the power and majesty of the cliffs, as well as the diverse flora and fauna that thrive in this unique environment.

Beyond hiking, Ireland offers a range of outdoor activities that allow you to experience its landscapes from different perspectives. Kayaking along the coast or on one of the country's many lakes provides a peaceful way to explore hidden coves and observe wildlife. The lakes of Killarney, Lough Corrib, and Lough Erne are popular destinations for paddlers, offering tranquil waters and stunning scenery.

Cycling enthusiasts will find plenty of routes to explore, from scenic coastal paths to challenging mountain trails. The Great Western Greenway in County Mayo is a dedicated cycling and walking trail that runs for 26 miles along a former railway line. This route offers a leisurely journey through some of

Ireland's most picturesque landscapes, with views of Clew Bay and the distant Nephin Mountains.

For those interested in rock climbing and bouldering, Ireland's varied geology provides numerous opportunities for adventure. The Burren in County Clare, with its unique limestone formations, is a popular destination for climbers, offering a range of routes for different skill levels. Similarly, the granite cliffs of Dalkey Quarry near Dublin provide a convenient location for climbing enthusiasts looking to test their skills.

Wildlife enthusiasts can take advantage of Ireland's rich biodiversity by participating in birdwatching or wildlife tours. The country's diverse habitats support a wide range of species, from seabirds and waders along the coast to raptors and songbirds in the mountains and forests. The Shannon Estuary, Wexford Slobs, and the islands of the west coast are renowned for their birdwatching opportunities, providing a chance to observe species such as puffins, gannets, and peregrine falcons in their natural habitats.

Ireland's outdoor adventures are not limited to land and water; the night sky offers its own wonders. The Kerry International Dark-Sky Reserve is one of the best places in the country to experience the majesty of the stars, free from the interference of artificial light. Here, on a clear night, you can marvel at the Milky Way and the constellations, gaining a deeper appreciation for the natural world both above and below.

Engaging in these outdoor activities provides more than just physical exercise; it offers a chance to connect with Ireland's landscapes and wildlife on a deeper level. Whether you're hiking a mountain trail, kayaking along a tranquil lake, or simply listening to the sounds of nature, these experiences create lasting memories and foster a sense of connection to the land.

As you plan your outdoor adventures in Ireland, consider the seasons and weather conditions, which can vary significantly across the country. The mild climate allows for year-round exploration, but being prepared with appropriate gear and clothing will enhance your experience. Respect for the environment and local communities is also essential, ensuring that these natural treasures are preserved for future generations to enjoy.

In Ireland, hiking trails and outdoor adventures beckon with promises of discovery and delight. The variety of landscapes, from mountains and lakes to coastlines and woodlands, offers endless opportunities for exploration and inspiration. As you embark on your journey, let the beauty of Ireland's natural world captivate your imagination, creating a tapestry of experiences and memories that will stay with you long after your adventure has ended.

4.5 National Parks and Wildlife

Ireland's national parks and wildlife reserves offer a glimpse into the country's breathtaking natural beauty and biodiversity. These protected areas serve as sanctuaries for a wide range of plant and animal species, showcasing the rich ecological diversity that thrives on the island. From the rugged mountains to the verdant forests, each national park tells a unique story of Ireland's natural history and provides opportunities for exploration, education, and conservation.

The jewel of Ireland's national parks is Killarney National Park, located in County Kerry. As the first national park established in Ireland, Killarney is a stunning tapestry of mountains, lakes, and woodlands. The park's centerpiece is the Lakes of Killarney, a trio of interconnected lakes that create a serene and picturesque landscape. The surrounding mountains, including the iconic MacGillycuddy's Reeks, provide a dramatic backdrop and offer numerous hiking trails for adventurers. The park is also home to the ancient oak and yew woodlands of the Muckross Peninsula, a haven for diverse wildlife, including Ireland's only remaining native herd of red deer.

Another gem in Ireland's national park system is the Burren National Park in County Clare. This unique landscape, characterized by its karst limestone formations, is a testament to the island's geological history. The Burren's stark beauty is complemented by a surprising array of flora and fauna, with over 70% of Ireland's native plant species found here. The park's diverse habitats, from limestone pavements to flower-rich meadows, support a variety of wildlife, including rare butterflies and birds of prey. Exploring the Burren provides a fascinating journey through a landscape shaped by both natural forces and human activity.

Glenveagh National Park, situated in County Donegal, offers a different kind of wilderness experience. Encompassing rugged mountains, pristine lakes, and vast expanses of moorland, Glenveagh is a remote and tranquil sanctuary. The park is home to the largest herd of red deer in Ireland, and its diverse habitats support a wide range of bird species, including the golden eagle, which has been successfully reintroduced to the area. At the heart of the park lies Glenveagh Castle, a 19th-century mansion surrounded by beautifully landscaped gardens, offering visitors a glimpse into the region's cultural heritage.

In County Tipperary, the expanse of wild beauty known as the Slieve Bloom Mountains provides a haven for outdoor enthusiasts. Though not designated as a national park, the Slieve Bloom Mountains Nature Reserve offers an extensive network of walking and cycling trails that wind through ancient woodlands and heath-covered hills. The reserve is home to a variety of wildlife, including red squirrels, pine martens, and a wide array of bird species. Its diverse habitats provide a rich tapestry of ecosystems that invite exploration and discovery.

The Wicklow Mountains National Park, located just south of Dublin, is the largest national park in Ireland. Its expansive landscapes encompass a range of environments, from heather-covered moorlands to deep glacial valleys and tranquil lakes. The park is home to a variety of wildlife, including sika deer, badgers, and peregrine falcons. The historic monastic site of Glendalough, nestled within the park, draws visitors from around the world with its ancient ruins and serene setting. The Wicklow Mountains offer a wealth of outdoor activities, from hiking and rock climbing to fishing and wildlife watching, providing a perfect escape into nature just a short distance from the bustling city.

The diversity of habitats within Ireland's national parks creates a rich tapestry of flora and fauna that is both fascinating and vital to the island's ecological health. These protected areas play a crucial role in conserving Ireland's biodiversity, offering refuge to species that might otherwise be threatened by habitat loss and human activity. Conservation efforts within the parks focus not only on protecting wildlife but also on preserving the unique landscapes and ecosystems that support them. This involves ongoing research and monitoring, habitat restoration projects, and community engagement to promote sustainable practices.

Visitors to Ireland's national parks are encouraged to engage with the natural world in a respectful and responsible manner. By following Leave No Trace principles, such as minimizing impact and respecting wildlife, visitors can help ensure that these natural treasures are preserved for future generations. Many parks offer educational programs and guided tours that provide deeper insights into the ecology and conservation efforts underway, fostering a greater appreciation for the natural world.

In addition to their ecological importance, Ireland's national parks and wildlife reserves offer a wealth of recreational opportunities. Hiking and walking trails allow visitors to explore the diverse landscapes at their own pace, while cycling routes provide an active way to experience the scenery. Water-based activities, such as kayaking and fishing, are available in many parks, offering a different perspective on the natural beauty of Ireland's lakes and rivers. For those interested in wildlife, birdwatching and nature photography provide a chance to observe and capture the rich biodiversity of these protected areas.

Experiencing the natural beauty of Ireland's national parks and wildlife reserves is not only about adventure and exploration; it is also a journey of connection and reflection. The serene landscapes and diverse habitats invite visitors to pause and appreciate the intricate web of life that thrives in these protected areas. Whether standing on a windswept mountain peak or walking through ancient woodlands, the sense of wonder and awe that these natural spaces inspire is a reminder of the importance of preserving and protecting the natural world.

Ireland's national parks and wildlife reserves are a testament to the country's commitment to conservation and the protection of its natural heritage. They offer a sanctuary for wildlife, a playground for outdoor enthusiasts, and a source of inspiration for all who visit. As stewards of these natural treasures, it is our responsibility to ensure that they remain vibrant and healthy, providing a legacy of beauty and biodiversity for generations to come. Engaging with Ireland's national parks is an invitation to explore, learn, and connect with the natural world in profound and meaningful ways.

4.6 Exploring the Aran Islands

Exploring the Aran Islands is like stepping into a world where time stands still, offering a glimpse into Ireland's rich cultural heritage and stunning natural beauty. Situated off the west coast of Ireland in Galway Bay, the islands consist of Inis Mór,

Inis Meáin, and Inis Oírr, each with its own unique character and charm. These islands are a sanctuary for Gaelic culture, with the Irish language widely spoken and traditional music and crafts thriving. The rugged landscapes, ancient ruins, and vibrant communities create an unforgettable experience for those who venture to these remote shores.

Inis Mór, the largest and most visited of the Aran Islands, is a treasure trove of history and natural wonders. The island's most iconic landmark is Dún Aonghasa, a prehistoric stone fort perched atop a 300-foot cliff overlooking the Atlantic Ocean. The fort's semicircular walls, dating back to the Bronze Age, offer a breathtaking vantage point and a sense of the island's ancient past. Walking the narrow paths leading to Dún Aonghasa, visitors are enveloped in the wild beauty of the island, with its limestone pavements, green fields, and expansive sea views.

Beyond Dún Aonghasa, Inis Mór is home to several other significant archaeological sites, including the Black Fort and the Seven Churches. The Black Fort, or Dún Dúchathair, is another ancient stone fort situated on a dramatic promontory, offering stunning views of the coastline. The Seven Churches, a monastic site dating back to the early Christian period, provides a glimpse into the island's spiritual heritage, with its ruined churches and ancient grave markers.

The island's landscape is characterized by its network of stone walls, which crisscross the fields and create a mosaic of small, enclosed plots. These walls, built by hand over centuries, are a testament to the ingenuity and resilience of the island's inhabitants. Cycling or walking along the quiet roads and paths of Inis Mór allows visitors to immerse themselves in this unique landscape, where wildflowers bloom and the sound of the sea is ever-present.

Inis Meáin, the middle island, offers a more tranquil and authentic experience, with fewer tourists and a strong emphasis on traditional culture. The island's landscape is a rugged tapestry of limestone karst, dotted with ancient ruins and traditional thatched cottages. Inis Meáin is renowned for its high-quality knitwear, with the Inis Meáin Knitting Company producing beautiful garments inspired by the island's natural colors and textures. Visitors can explore the island's many archaeological sites, including the ancient fort of Dún Chonchúir and the early Christian church of St. Ciarán's.

The island's cultural heritage is celebrated through its vibrant arts scene, with local artists drawing inspiration from the landscape and its history. The Inis Meáin Arts Centre hosts exhibitions and events throughout the year, showcasing the work of both local and visiting artists. The island's small, close-knit community offers a warm welcome to visitors, providing an opportunity to experience the traditional way of life and the enduring spirit of the islanders.

Inis Oírr, the smallest of the Aran Islands, is a charming and picturesque destination, with its sandy beaches, colorful cottages, and lively cultural scene. The island's main attraction is O'Brien's Castle, a 14th-century fortress perched on a hill, offering panoramic views of the island and the surrounding sea. The castle's ruins are a reminder of the island's turbulent history, with its strategic location making it a target for invaders over the centuries.

Inis Oírr is also home to the Plassey shipwreck, famously featured in the opening credits of the television series "Father Ted." The rusting remains of the cargo ship, which ran aground on the island in 1960, have become an iconic symbol of the island's rugged coastline and maritime heritage. Walking along the island's beaches and cliffs, visitors can witness the power and beauty of the Atlantic Ocean, with its crashing waves and ever-changing skies.

The island's cultural life is vibrant and welcoming, with traditional music sessions and events held regularly in the local pubs and community centers. The islanders' love of music and storytelling is infectious, creating a warm and inviting atmosphere for visitors. Inis Oírr also hosts an annual arts festival, celebrating the island's creative spirit and providing a platform for local and international artists to share their work.

Traveling to the Aran Islands is an adventure in itself, with ferries operating from the mainland ports of Doolin and Rossaveal. The journey across Galway Bay offers stunning views of the Connemara coastline and the Cliffs of Moher, setting the stage for the islands' dramatic landscapes. For those seeking a unique perspective, flights are also available from Connemara Airport, providing a bird's-eye view of the islands' rugged beauty.

Exploring the Aran Islands offers more than just breathtaking scenery and ancient sites; it provides a window into a way of life that has endured for centuries. The islands' commitment to preserving their cultural heritage and natural environment is evident in the strong sense of community and pride among the inhabitants. Visitors are encouraged to engage with the local culture, whether by attending a traditional music session, participating in a craft workshop, or simply enjoying a conversation with an islander.

The islands' unique landscapes and rich history create a sense of wonder and discovery, inviting visitors to slow down and savor the experience. Whether cycling along the quiet roads of Inis Mór, exploring the rugged terrain of Inis Meáin, or soaking in the vibrant culture of Inis Oírr, the Aran Islands offer an unforgettable journey into the heart of Ireland's natural and cultural heritage. The islands' timeless beauty and enduring spirit leave a lasting impression, creating memories and connections that resonate long after the journey has ended.

4.7 Local Legends and Folklore

Ireland's local legends and folklore form an integral part of its cultural tapestry, weaving tales of mystery, magic, and the supernatural into the very fabric of everyday life. These stories, passed down through generations, capture the imagination and provide insight into the values, fears, and hopes of the Irish people. From ancient myths of heroic warriors and mystical creatures to ghostly apparitions and enchanted landscapes, the folklore of Ireland offers a rich and captivating narrative that continues to resonate today.

One of the most enduring legends is that of the Tuatha Dé Danann, a mythical race of supernatural beings said to have inhabited Ireland before the arrival of humans. According to legend, they descended from the skies in ships shrouded in mist, bringing with them powerful magic and advanced knowledge. The Tuatha Dé Danann were believed to possess great wisdom and skill in arts and crafts, and they were revered as the gods and goddesses of ancient Ireland. Their stories are chronicled in the Lebor Gabála Érenn, or the Book of Invasions, which tells of their battles against the Fomorians, a race of malevolent giants. Although eventually defeated, the Tuatha Dé Danann are said to have retreated into the Otherworld, becoming the fairies and spirits that continue to inhabit the land.

The legend of Cú Chulainn, a hero from the Ulster Cycle of Irish mythology, embodies the archetypal warrior ethos. Renowned for his superhuman strength and martial prowess, Cú Chulainn's exploits are the stuff of legend. His most famous tale, the Táin Bó Cúailnge, recounts his defense of Ulster against the armies of Connacht, led by Queen Medb, in a cattle raid that becomes an epic battle. Cú Chulainn's story highlights themes of bravery, loyalty, and the tragic consequences of pride, cementing his status as one of Ireland's most iconic mythological figures.

Folklore also abounds with tales of the banshee, a ghostly female figure whose mournful wail is said to foretell death. The banshee is often depicted as an old woman with long, flowing hair and a pale, spectral appearance. Her eerie cry is believed to be a lament for the deceased, and families with ancient Irish lineage are said to be particularly susceptible to her warnings. The banshee's presence in folklore underscores the deep connection between the living and the spirit world in Irish culture, reflecting a belief in the continuity of life beyond death.

The leprechaun, perhaps Ireland's most famous folkloric character, is a mischievous fairy known for his love of gold and trickery. Often depicted as a small, bearded man dressed in green, the leprechaun is said to guard hidden pots of gold at the end of rainbows. Capturing a leprechaun is thought to grant three wishes, but his cunning nature ensures that such endeavors rarely succeed. The leprechaun's playful antics and association with luck have made him a beloved symbol of Irish folklore, embodying the wit and resourcefulness that are celebrated in Irish culture.

The selkie, a creature found in the folklore of coastal communities, is said to be a seal that can shed its skin to become human. These enchanting beings are often depicted as beautiful men or women who can captivate the hearts of mortals. However, if a selkie's skin is taken or hidden by a human, the selkie is bound to remain on land until it is returned. The tales of selkies speak to the deep connection between the people of Ireland and the sea, highlighting themes of longing, transformation, and the tension between freedom and captivity.

Ghost stories and supernatural occurrences are an integral part of Ireland's folklore, with many locations across the country reputed to be haunted by spirits. One such place is Leap Castle in County Offaly, often described as the most haunted castle in Ireland. Built in the 13th century, Leap Castle has a dark and turbulent history, with tales of betrayal, murder, and family feuds. The castle is said to be home to several spirits, including the terrifying Elemental, a malevolent entity that reportedly exudes a foul odor and instills fear in those who encounter it. Visitors and paranormal investigators have reported strange occurrences and sightings, adding to the castle's eerie reputation.

The story of the Children of Lir is a poignant tale of transformation and loss that has captured the hearts of many. According to legend, the four children of Lir, a powerful chieftain, were transformed into swans by their jealous stepmother, Aoife. Condemned to spend 900 years in this form, the children were forced to wander the lakes and rivers of Ireland until the curse was finally broken. The tale of the Children of Lir is a reflection on the themes of family, resilience, and the enduring nature of love, with the swans becoming a symbol of beauty and grace in Irish folklore.

Ireland's folklore is also rich with stories of sacred wells, enchanted forests, and fairy forts—ancient ringforts believed to be inhabited by fairies. These sites are often regarded with reverence and caution, as disturbing them is thought to bring misfortune. The belief in fairies and the Otherworld is deeply ingrained in Irish culture, influencing customs and traditions for generations. Many people still leave offerings at sacred sites, seeking protection or favor from the fairies and honoring the ancient spirits of the land.

The oral tradition of storytelling has played a vital role in preserving Ireland's folklore, with seanchaí, or traditional storytellers, passing down tales from one generation to the next. These stories, often shared during gatherings and festivals, serve as a means of connecting the community and keeping the cultural heritage alive. The seanchaí's role is deeply respected, as they are seen as the custodians of history, wisdom, and imagination.

In contemporary Ireland, folklore continues to inspire writers, artists, and musicians, who draw on these ancient stories to create new works that resonate with modern audiences. From literature and film to music and visual arts, the influence of folklore is evident in the creative expression of Irish culture. This enduring legacy ensures that the tales of old remain vibrant and relevant, capturing the imagination of people both within Ireland and beyond its shores.

Local legends and folklore offer a window into the soul of Ireland, providing a rich tapestry of stories that reflect the island's history, landscapes, and people. These tales, whether of heroic deeds, ghostly apparitions, or mischievous fairies, capture the essence of what it means to be Irish, celebrating the imagination, resilience, and spirit of the culture. By exploring these stories, one gains a deeper understanding of the values and beliefs that have shaped Ireland, creating a connection that transcends time and place.

CHAPTER 5: CONNECTING WITH LOCAL CULTURE

5.1 Traditional Irish Music and Dance

Traditional Irish music and dance are vibrant expressions of Ireland's rich cultural heritage, capturing the spirit and soul of the island through rhythm, melody, and movement. These art forms, deeply rooted in the oral tradition, have been passed down through generations, evolving over time while maintaining their distinctive character. From lively jigs and reels to soulful ballads and sean-nós dance, the music and dance of Ireland offer a captivating journey into the heart of its people and their history.

The origins of traditional Irish music can be traced back centuries, with influences from Celtic, Norse, and Anglo-Saxon cultures interweaving to create a unique and distinctive sound. Central to this music is the use of traditional instruments, each contributing its own timbre and flavor to the ensemble. The fiddle, a staple of Irish music, is known for its expressive range and ability to convey both joy and melancholy. The uilleann pipes, with their haunting and ethereal tones, add a distinctive voice that is uniquely Irish. The bodhrán, a frame drum played with a stick called a tipper, provides the rhythmic foundation, driving the music forward with its pulsating beats. Other instruments, such as the tin whistle, flute, and accordion, further enrich the tapestry of sound, creating a dynamic and engaging musical experience.

Traditional Irish music is often performed in sessions, informal gatherings where musicians come together to share tunes and songs. These sessions, held in pubs and community centers across Ireland, are more than just performances; they are social events where musicians and listeners alike connect through a shared love of music. The repertoire includes a wide variety of tunes, from lively dance tunes like jigs, reels, and hornpipes to slower airs and ballads that tell stories of love, loss, and adventure. The communal nature of sessions fosters a sense of camaraderie and tradition, with musicians learning tunes by ear and passing them on to the next generation.

Irish dance, like its musical counterpart, is an integral part of the island's cultural identity. The origins of Irish dance are shrouded in mystery, but it is believed to have evolved from ancient Celtic and Druidic rituals. Over time, it developed into distinct styles and forms, each with its own steps, rhythms, and regional variations. The most well-known form is Irish step dance, characterized by its precise footwork, rigid upper body, and intricate patterns. This style gained international fame through shows like "Riverdance" and "Lord of the Dance," showcasing the athleticism and artistry of Irish dancers to audiences around the world.

Another important style is sean-nós dance, a more relaxed and improvisational form that emphasizes personal expression and musicality. Unlike step dance, sean-nós dancers keep their arms loose and use subtle movements to interpret the music, often dancing solo or in small groups. This style is particularly popular in the west of Ireland, where it is celebrated for its connection to the Irish language and traditional culture.

Ceili dancing, a social form of dance, brings people together in group formations and is often performed at gatherings and festivals. These dances, which include set dances and figure dances, are lively and engaging, encouraging participation and interaction among dancers. The emphasis on community and connection makes ceili dancing a cherished aspect of Irish social life, fostering a sense of belonging and shared heritage.

The preservation and promotion of traditional Irish music and dance are supported by organizations such as Comhaltas Ceoltóirí Éireann, which was founded in 1951 to promote Irish culture and heritage. Through festivals, workshops, and competitions, Comhaltas provides opportunities for musicians and dancers of all ages to learn, perform, and celebrate their cultural roots. The annual Fleadh Cheoil na hÉireann, organized by Comhaltas, is the largest festival of Irish music and dance in the world, attracting thousands of participants and spectators from across the globe.

For beginners interested in exploring traditional Irish music and dance, there are numerous resources and opportunities available. Many communities offer classes and workshops for aspiring musicians and dancers, providing instruction in the fundamentals of playing instruments or learning dance steps. Attending sessions and ceili dances is a great way to immerse oneself in the culture, meet fellow enthusiasts, and gain a deeper understanding of the traditions.

It's important to approach learning with an open mind and a willingness to listen and observe. Traditional Irish music and dance are deeply rooted in improvisation and personal expression, allowing individuals to develop their own style and interpretation. Listening to recordings of renowned musicians and watching performances by accomplished dancers can provide inspiration and insight into the nuances of the art forms.

Participation in festivals and competitions, such as the aforementioned Fleadh Cheoil, can also be a rewarding experience, offering the chance to showcase one's skills and connect with a wider community of enthusiasts. These events celebrate the talent and creativity of musicians and dancers, fostering an environment of encouragement and support.

In contemporary Ireland, traditional music and dance continue to evolve and thrive, with many artists blending traditional elements with modern influences to create innovative and exciting new works. This fusion of old and new ensures that the traditions remain relevant and dynamic, appealing to audiences both within Ireland and beyond its shores. Artists such as The Chieftains, Clannad, and Riverdance have played a significant role in popularizing Irish music and dance on the global stage, introducing these vibrant art forms to new generations.

Traditional Irish music and dance offer a window into the soul of Ireland, capturing the essence of its people, their history, and their enduring spirit. These art forms are more than just entertainment; they are a means of preserving and celebrating a rich cultural heritage that continues to inspire and unite people across the world. Whether through the joyous sounds of a fiddle tune or the rhythmic footwork of a dancer, the music and dance of Ireland invite all to join in the celebration of life, community, and the timeless stories that connect us all.

5.2 Pubs and the Art of Conversation

The Irish pub is more than just a place to enjoy a pint; it is a cultural institution, a gathering place where the art of conversation flourishes. Steeped in tradition and history, pubs are integral to the social fabric of Ireland, offering a warm and welcoming atmosphere where locals and visitors alike can connect, share stories, and engage in lively discussions. The pub is a microcosm of Irish society, reflecting its values, humor, and love of storytelling.

Walking into an Irish pub is like stepping into a world where time slows down, and the outside world fades away. The warm glow of the fire, the clink of glasses, and the soft hum of conversation create an inviting ambiance that beckons patrons to relax and unwind. The décor often reflects the character of the establishment, with dark wood, vintage photographs, and memorabilia adorning the walls, each piece with its own story to tell. The bar, a central feature, serves as a stage where the ritual of pouring a perfectly crafted pint unfolds, an art form in itself.

At the heart of the pub experience is the art of conversation, a cherished tradition that has been honed over centuries. The

Irish have a natural gift for storytelling, and the pub provides the perfect setting for this talent to shine. Conversations in Irish pubs are rich and varied, ranging from light-hearted banter to deep philosophical debates. The topics are as diverse as the patrons themselves, encompassing politics, sports, music, history, and everything in between.

Central to these conversations is the concept of "craic," an Irish term that embodies fun, enjoyment, and good company. The craic is what transforms a simple gathering into a memorable experience, where laughter and camaraderie flow as freely as the drinks. It is the essence of what makes Irish pubs special, a reminder that the joy of human connection is often found in the simplest of interactions.

The role of the bartender, or "publican," is pivotal in fostering the atmosphere of the pub. More than just a server of drinks, the publican is a confidant, mediator, and storyteller, skilled in the delicate art of conversation. They know their patrons by name, remember their favorite drinks, and are adept at drawing people into the fold, making newcomers feel like old friends. The publican's ability to weave stories and anecdotes into the fabric of the evening adds depth and texture to the pub experience, creating a sense of community and belonging.

Pubs are also venues for traditional Irish music, an integral part of the cultural experience. The sound of fiddles, flutes, and bodhráns fills the air, creating a lively backdrop for conversation. Music sessions, often impromptu, bring people together, encouraging participation and interaction. The shared experience of listening to music and joining in song fosters a sense of unity and connection, transcending language and cultural barriers.

For beginners seeking to engage in the art of conversation in an Irish pub, there are a few key principles to keep in mind. First and foremost, approach interactions with an open mind and a willingness to listen. The beauty of pub conversations lies in their spontaneity and diversity, and being receptive to different perspectives enriches the experience. Humor is a vital component of Irish conversation, so don't be afraid to share a joke or a light-hearted story. The Irish have a keen appreciation for wit and wordplay, and a well-timed quip can quickly break the ice.

Respect for others is paramount, and conversations should be approached with a spirit of inclusivity and equality. The informal nature of pub interactions allows for a free exchange of ideas, but it is important to remain respectful and considerate, even when discussing contentious topics. The ability to engage in spirited debate without animosity is a hallmark of the Irish conversational style.

Storytelling is an art that can be cultivated, and the pub provides the ideal setting to hone this skill. Sharing personal stories or anecdotes can create a connection with others, inviting them to share their own experiences in return. The rhythm and cadence of storytelling, coupled with expressive language and vivid detail, can captivate an audience and transform a simple tale into a memorable narrative.

Participation in a music session, whether by clapping along, singing, or even playing an instrument, can be a wonderful way to immerse oneself in the culture and engage with others. The communal nature of these sessions encourages camaraderie and collaboration, creating an atmosphere of shared enjoyment and celebration.

Pubs also serve as important community hubs, hosting events and gatherings that bring people together for various causes and celebrations. From charity fundraisers to quiz nights and sports viewings, pubs provide a space for collective experiences that strengthen community bonds. These events offer additional opportunities for conversation and connection, allowing individuals to engage with others in meaningful ways.

In contemporary Ireland, the pub remains a vital part of social life, evolving to meet the needs and preferences of a changing society. While the traditional elements of the pub experience endure, many establishments have embraced modern influences, offering a diverse range of craft beers, artisanal spirits, and innovative food offerings. This fusion of tradition and innovation ensures that the pub remains relevant and appealing to a new generation of patrons.

The art of conversation in Irish pubs is a celebration of human connection, a reminder of the importance of community, and the joy of shared experiences. It is a testament to the enduring power of storytelling, humor, and camaraderie to bring people together and create lasting memories. As an embodiment of Ireland's cultural heritage, the pub invites all who enter to partake in the rich tapestry of conversation and connection that defines the Irish spirit.

5.3 Festivals and Cultural Events

Ireland's festivals and cultural events offer a vibrant tapestry of celebration, showcasing the country's rich heritage, traditions, and creative spirit. These gatherings bring communities together and attract visitors from around the world, eager to experience the unique blend of history, music, dance, and art that defines Irish culture. From ancient rituals to modern spectacles, the festivals of Ireland capture the essence of its people, creating moments of joy, reflection, and connection.

St. Patrick's Day, celebrated on the 17th of March, is perhaps the most renowned of all Irish festivals. Commemorating the patron saint of Ireland, this day is marked by parades, music, and revelry. Cities and towns across the country come alive with vibrant displays of green, as people dress in festive attire and take to the streets. While Dublin's St. Patrick's Festival is a highlight, with its grand parade and cultural events, smaller towns offer their own unique charm, celebrating with local traditions and community gatherings. The festival's global reach has made it an emblem of Irish identity, celebrated in cities around the world.

The Fleadh Cheoil na hÉireann, or Festival of Music, is the pinnacle of traditional Irish music and dance. Organized by Comhaltas Ceoltóirí Éireann, this annual event brings together musicians and dancers of all ages for a week of competitions, sessions, and concerts. The host town becomes a bustling hub of activity, with impromptu music sessions spilling out onto the streets, and the air filled with the sounds of fiddles, flutes, and bodhráns. The Fleadh Cheoil is a testament to the vibrancy of Irish traditional arts, fostering a sense of community and preserving cultural heritage for future generations.

Ireland also boasts a rich literary tradition, celebrated through events like the Dublin International Literary Festival. This gathering of writers, poets, and readers offers a platform for discussions, readings, and workshops, exploring the written word in all its forms. The festival attracts renowned authors and emerging voices, providing an opportunity for literary enthusiasts to engage with their favorite writers and discover new talent. With its focus on storytelling and creativity, the festival underscores Ireland's enduring love for literature and its impact on global culture.

For those seeking a taste of Irish folklore and mythology, the Puck Fair in Killorglin, County Kerry, presents a unique spectacle. One of Ireland's oldest festivals, its origins are shrouded in legend, with tales of ancient kings and pagan rituals. The centerpiece of the fair is the crowning of a wild goat as king, symbolizing the town's connection to nature and its agricultural roots. The three-day event features horse fairs, parades, music, and dance, creating a lively and colorful celebration that draws visitors from near and far.

The Galway International Arts Festival is a dynamic showcase of creativity, spanning theatre, music, visual arts, and more. Held annually in July, the festival transforms the city into a vibrant cultural playground, with performances and installations taking place across various venues. International and local artists converge to present innovative works, pushing the boundaries of artistic expression. The festival's diverse program offers something for everyone, from avant-garde performances to family-friendly events, reflecting the city's spirit of inclusivity and artistic exploration.

Halloween, or Samhain, is deeply rooted in Ireland's Celtic heritage, marking the transition from the harvest season to winter. The ancient festival has evolved into a modern celebration, with events such as the Bram Stoker Festival in Dublin paying homage to the author of "Dracula" and exploring themes of horror and the supernatural. The festival features theatrical performances, film screenings, and interactive experiences, inviting participants to delve into the darker side of Irish folklore. Traditional customs, such as carving turnip lanterns and lighting bonfires, continue to be practiced, preserving the connection to Ireland's ancient past.

The Rose of Tralee International Festival is a celebration of Irish culture and heritage, attracting participants from across the Irish diaspora. Held in Tralee, County Kerry, the festival culminates in the selection of the "Rose," a young woman chosen for her personality, intelligence, and cultural connection. The event includes parades, concerts, and street entertainment, creating a festive atmosphere that celebrates the global Irish community. The festival's emphasis on cultural exchange and friendship highlights the enduring bonds that connect Ireland to its people worldwide.

For those interested in contemporary art and performance, the Dublin Fringe Festival offers a platform for emerging artists to showcase their work. With a focus on innovation and experimentation, the festival features a diverse range of performances, from theatre and dance to spoken word and multimedia installations. The Fringe Festival challenges traditional boundaries, encouraging artists to take risks and push creative limits. This celebration of artistic freedom and expression has become a fixture of Dublin's cultural calendar, attracting audiences eager to experience cutting-edge work.

The Listowel Writers' Week, held in County Kerry, is Ireland's oldest literary festival, celebrating the joy of writing and reading. The event brings together authors, poets, and playwrights for a series of workshops, readings, and discussions, fostering a love of literature and the written word. The festival's intimate setting allows for meaningful interactions between writers and readers, creating a space for inspiration and creativity. As a testament to Ireland's rich literary heritage, the Writers' Week continues to nurture and support the literary community.

Ireland's festivals and cultural events offer a window into the heart of the nation, showcasing its rich traditions, creativity, and community spirit. These gatherings provide an opportunity for people to come together, share experiences, and celebrate the diverse tapestry of Irish culture. Whether through the joyous revelry of St. Patrick's Day, the haunting melodies of the Fleadh Cheoil, or the innovative performances of the Dublin Fringe Festival, Ireland's cultural events invite all to partake in the vibrant and enduring spirit of the island. Through these celebrations, the stories, music, and traditions of Ireland continue to inspire and connect people across the world.

5.4 Gaelic Language and Traditions

The Gaelic language, or Gaeilge, is more than just a means of communication; it is a cornerstone of Irish identity, embodying the history, culture, and traditions of the island. As one of the oldest languages in Europe, Gaelic has survived centuries of change, conflict, and colonization, maintaining its unique character and significance. Today, efforts to preserve and revive the language are intertwined with a broader appreciation of Irish traditions, fostering a renewed sense of pride and connection to the past.

Gaelic's origins can be traced back to the Celtic tribes that settled in Ireland around 500 BC. Over the centuries, it evolved into Old Irish, Middle Irish, and eventually Modern Irish, reflecting the linguistic shifts and influences that shaped its development. Despite facing periods of decline, particularly during British rule when English was imposed as the dominant language, Gaelic persisted as a symbol of resistance and cultural resilience.

The language's survival owes much to the efforts of the Gaelic Revival in the late 19th and early 20th centuries. This cultural movement sought to revive Irish language, literature, and traditions, countering the effects of Anglicization. Organizations such as the Gaelic League played a pivotal role in promoting Irish language education and encouraging its use in everyday life. This renaissance laid the groundwork for the language's inclusion as an official language of the Irish Free State in 1922, bolstering its status and visibility.

In modern Ireland, the promotion and preservation of Gaelic are supported by various initiatives and institutions. The Gaeltacht regions—areas where Gaelic is the primary spoken language—serve as vital bastions of linguistic and cultural preservation. These regions, located mainly in the west of Ireland, offer immersive experiences for learners and visitors keen to engage with the language and its associated traditions. In addition, schools known as Gaelscoileanna provide education primarily through Gaelic, fostering fluency and cultural awareness among young people.

For beginners interested in learning Gaelic, there are numerous resources and opportunities available. Language courses, both in-person and online, cater to different levels of proficiency, allowing learners to progress at their own pace. Engaging with Gaelic media, such as radio, television, and literature, can enhance language skills and provide valuable insights into Irish culture and society. Immersion experiences, whether through visits to the Gaeltacht or participation in language-focused events, offer practical opportunities to practice speaking and listening in real-life contexts.

The importance of Gaelic extends beyond its linguistic value; it is inextricably linked to Ireland's rich tapestry of traditions and folklore. The language serves as a vehicle for preserving ancient myths, stories, and customs, offering a window into Ireland's past. From tales of legendary heroes like Fionn mac Cumhaill to the enchanting poetry of the Fianna, Gaelic literature captures the imagination and provides a deeper understanding of the cultural heritage that shapes Ireland.

One such tradition is the art of sean-nós singing, a highly ornamented and emotive style of unaccompanied vocal music. Sung in Gaelic, sean-nós songs often tell stories of love, loss, and the landscape, reflecting the deep connection between the people and their environment. This style of singing is characterized by its free rhythm and expressive phrasing, allowing singers to infuse their performances with personal interpretation and emotion. Sean-nós singing is celebrated in festivals and gatherings across Ireland, offering listeners a profound and moving experience.

The Irish tradition of storytelling, or scéalaíocht, is another cultural practice that finds its roots in the Gaelic language. Storytellers, or seanchaí, have long been revered as custodians of history and folklore, passing down tales through generations. These narratives, often imbued with humor, wisdom, and moral lessons, serve as a means of connecting communities and preserving collective memory. The seanchaí's artful use of language and vivid imagery brings stories to life, captivating audiences and keeping the oral tradition alive.

Gaelic sports, such as hurling and Gaelic football, are integral to Ireland's cultural identity, with their origins deeply rooted in Gaelic tradition. Governed by the Gaelic Athletic Association (GAA), these sports are celebrated for their fast-paced action, skill, and community spirit. Hurling, often described as the fastest field sport in the world, showcases the athleticism and precision of its players, while Gaelic football combines elements of soccer and rugby in a uniquely Irish game. These sports are more than just recreational activities; they are a means of fostering local pride and camaraderie, with clubs serving as focal points for community involvement.

The celebration of traditional Irish festivals, such as Bealtaine and Samhain, is closely linked to Gaelic culture and the ancient Celtic calendar. These festivals mark the changing seasons and are steeped in rituals that honor the cycles of nature. Bealtaine, celebrated on May 1st, heralds the arrival of summer with bonfires, music, and dance, symbolizing renewal and fertility. Samhain, the precursor to Halloween, marks the end of the harvest season and the onset of winter, with customs that reflect themes of transition and reflection. These festivals provide a tangible connection to Ireland's pagan past and offer opportunities to engage with traditional customs and practices.

The revival of Gaelic arts and crafts, such as weaving, pottery, and metalwork, also plays a significant role in preserving cultural heritage. Artisans draw inspiration from ancient Celtic motifs and techniques, creating contemporary pieces that celebrate traditional craftsmanship. These crafts serve as expressions of identity and creativity, bridging the gap between past and present.

The Gaelic language and its associated traditions offer a profound connection to Ireland's cultural heritage, embodying the values, stories, and spirit of its people. Through language, music, storytelling, and customs, the richness of Gaelic culture continues to inspire and resonate. For those who seek to explore and embrace this heritage, the journey is one of discovery, learning, and appreciation—a path that leads to a deeper understanding of what it means to be part of the Irish cultural tapestry. Through the preservation and celebration of Gaelic traditions, the legacy of the past is woven into the fabric of contemporary life, ensuring that the stories and voices of Ireland endure for generations to come.

5.5 Engaging with Locals

Engaging with locals in Ireland offers a unique and enriching experience, providing insights into the culture and daily life of the island. The Irish are renowned for their warmth, hospitality, and storytelling prowess, making interactions with them both enjoyable and enlightening. Whether you're visiting a bustling city or a tranquil village, connecting with local people can deepen your understanding of the traditions, values, and rhythms of Irish life.

The key to successful engagement lies in genuine curiosity and openness. The Irish are naturally conversational, and they appreciate when visitors take an interest in their culture and way of life. Initiating a conversation with a friendly greeting or a simple question can open the door to a rewarding exchange. Topics such as local history, sports, or current events often serve as excellent starting points and reveal the passions and concerns of the community. Listening actively and showing appreciation for their stories and perspectives can foster a sense of connection and mutual respect.

Ireland's pub culture provides an ideal setting for engaging with locals. Pubs are more than just places for a drink; they are social hubs where people gather to relax, share news, and enjoy music. Joining a local pub session allows you to experience this convivial atmosphere firsthand. You might find yourself drawn into discussions ranging from the latest Gaelic football match to the nuances of traditional music. Participating in these conversations, while respecting the informal and inclusive nature of the setting, can offer a glimpse into the heart of Irish life.

Community events and festivals also present opportunities for meaningful interactions. Whether it's a local fair, a music festival, or a cultural celebration, these gatherings bring people together and showcase the vibrancy of community life. Volunteering at such events can be a rewarding way to contribute and connect, allowing you to meet locals who share a common interest or passion. Additionally, attending workshops or demonstrations related to traditional crafts or skills can provide insights into the cultural heritage of the area while facilitating conversations with those who carry on these traditions.

Exploring the countryside and smaller towns can offer its own set of rewards. In these settings, the pace of life is often slower, and people may have more time to engage in conversation. Taking the time to visit local shops, markets, or cafes can lead to chance encounters and spontaneous exchanges. Asking for recommendations on local attractions, places to eat, or hidden gems can reveal not only insider tips but also stories and anecdotes that add depth to your experience.

One of the most meaningful ways to engage with locals is through shared experiences. Joining a sports club, taking a class, or participating in a local interest group can offer opportunities to bond over common activities. Whether it's learning to play a traditional Irish instrument, taking part in a hiking group, or joining a Gaelic games team, these experiences provide a natural context for building relationships and gaining insights into the community's values and dynamics.

Respect for local customs and etiquette is essential when engaging with locals. Being mindful of social norms, such as greeting people with a handshake or respecting personal space, can ease interactions and demonstrate cultural sensitivity. The Irish have a reputation for humor and wit, and a willingness to share a laugh or a light-hearted story can enhance social bonds. However, it's important to be aware of the context and avoid sensitive topics unless they are introduced by the local person.

The rich tapestry of the Irish language and dialects adds another layer to engaging with locals. While English is widely spoken, Gaelic is an integral part of Ireland's cultural identity. Learning a few basic Gaelic phrases can show respect for the language and its heritage, often leading to positive reactions from locals. Additionally, being attuned to regional dialects and expressions can enhance your understanding of the nuances of conversation and foster a deeper connection.

For those seeking to engage with locals on a deeper level, the concept of "meitheal" offers a meaningful approach. Rooted in the tradition of communal cooperation, meitheal involves neighbors coming together to help each other with tasks such as farming, building, or community projects. Participating in or supporting these communal efforts fosters a sense of solidarity and shared purpose, reflecting the values of community support and collaboration that are central to Irish life.

Capturing these interactions through journaling or photography can serve as a personal record of your experiences and the connections you've made. Reflecting on these moments can deepen your appreciation for the cultural exchange and the friendships formed along the way. Sharing these stories with others, whether through social media, blogs, or personal conversations, can extend the impact of your engagement and inspire others to seek similar connections.

Engaging with locals in Ireland offers a wealth of opportunities to explore the culture, build relationships, and gain a deeper understanding of the island's people and traditions. Through genuine curiosity, openness, and respect, these interactions can enrich your experience and create lasting memories. Whether through conversation, shared activities, or participation in community life, the connections made with locals are an integral part of the Irish experience, providing insights and stories that linger long after your visit. In the end, it is these human connections that make travel meaningful and transformative, bridging cultures and fostering a sense of global community.

5.6 Art and Literature in Ireland

Ireland has long been celebrated for its rich tapestry of art and literature, a legacy that has shaped the cultural identity of the island and resonated far beyond its shores. Steeped in history and tradition, Irish art and literature offer a window into the soul of the nation, revealing its struggles, triumphs, and enduring spirit. From ancient Celtic expressions to contemporary works, the creative output of Ireland is as diverse as it is profound.

The roots of Irish art can be traced back to prehistoric times, with the intricate stone carvings at sites such as Newgrange providing a glimpse into the artistic sensibilities of early inhabitants. These ancient motifs evolved over the centuries, culminating in the exquisite craftsmanship of the Celtic period. The illuminated manuscripts of the early medieval era, most notably the Book of Kells, stand as testaments to the skill and creativity of Irish monks. With their elaborate designs and vivid colors, these works remain some of the finest examples of medieval art.

As Ireland transitioned into the modern era, its art continued to evolve, reflecting the social and political changes of the time. The 19th century saw the emergence of the Irish landscape tradition, with artists like Paul Henry capturing the rugged beauty of the west of Ireland. These works, characterized by their atmospheric depictions and subtle use of color, conveyed a sense of place that resonated with the national consciousness.

In the realm of literature, Ireland's contribution is equally significant. The oral tradition of storytelling, deeply embedded in Gaelic culture, provided fertile ground for the development of a rich literary heritage. The works of early bards and poets, such as those found in the Táin Bó Cúailnge, laid the foundation for a literary tradition that would flourish in the centuries to come.

The late 19th and early 20th centuries marked a golden age for Irish literature, with figures such as W.B. Yeats, James Joyce, and Samuel Beckett achieving international acclaim. Yeats, with his evocative poetry steeped in myth and mysticism, captured the imagination of readers worldwide. Joyce's groundbreaking works, including "Ulysses," revolutionized the novel form, utilizing stream-of-consciousness techniques to delve into the complexities of the human psyche. Beckett, a master of minimalist prose and existential themes, challenged conventional narratives and remains a towering figure in modern literature.

The legacy of these literary giants continues to inspire contemporary writers, who explore diverse themes and genres while maintaining a connection to their cultural roots. Contemporary Irish literature is marked by a multiplicity of voices, reflecting the country's evolving identity and global outlook.

The arts in Ireland have also benefited from a robust infrastructure of support and promotion. Institutions such as the Irish Museum of Modern Art and the National Gallery of Ireland play a crucial role in preserving and showcasing the nation's artistic heritage. These venues provide a platform for established and emerging artists to exhibit their work, fostering a dynamic cultural landscape that encourages innovation and exploration.

The annual Galway International Arts Festival exemplifies the vibrancy of Ireland's contemporary arts scene. This multidisciplinary event brings together artists from around the world, offering a diverse program of theatre, music, visual arts, and more. By facilitating collaboration and exchange, the festival contributes to the ongoing dialogue between Irish artists and the global community.

In the realm of literature, the Dublin International Literary Festival serves as a focal point for writers and readers alike. This gathering celebrates the written word in all its forms, offering discussions, readings, and workshops that engage with both classic and contemporary works. By connecting authors with audiences, the festival nurtures a love of literature and encourages the exploration of new ideas and narratives.

For beginners eager to immerse themselves in Irish art and literature, there are several practical steps to take. Visiting galleries and museums across the country provides an opportunity to experience firsthand the breadth and depth of Ireland's artistic output. Engaging with local artists and attending exhibitions can offer insights into the creative process and the themes that inspire their work.

Reading Irish literature, both classic and contemporary, is a rewarding way to explore the nation's literary heritage. From the lyrical poetry of Seamus Heaney to the compelling narratives of Anne Enright, Irish writers offer a wealth of stories that resonate with universal themes of identity, love, and the human condition. Participating in book clubs or literary events can further enhance this experience, providing a forum for discussion and reflection.

For those interested in exploring the intersection of art and literature, workshops and courses offer opportunities to engage with both disciplines in a supportive environment. Whether through creative writing classes or art workshops, these experiences encourage participants to develop their skills and express themselves creatively, drawing inspiration from Ireland's rich cultural heritage.

Ireland's art and literature are integral to its identity, offering a lens through which to view the country's history, values, and aspirations. By engaging with these creative expressions, one can gain a deeper appreciation for the complexity and beauty of Irish culture. The stories and images that emerge from this vibrant tradition continue to captivate and inspire, inviting us to reflect on our own experiences and the world around us. Through the arts, Ireland shares its unique voice, contributing to a global dialogue that celebrates diversity and creativity in all its forms.

CHAPTER 6: CULINARY JOURNEY THROUGH IRELAND

6.1 Traditional Irish Dishes

The culinary landscape of Ireland is as rich and varied as its history, offering a delightful array of traditional dishes that have been passed down through generations. Rooted in hearty, wholesome ingredients, Irish cuisine reflects the island's agricultural heritage and its people's resilience and ingenuity. From savory stews to sweet treats, these dishes provide a taste of Ireland's past while continuing to delight palates in the present.

At the heart of traditional Irish cooking lies the humble potato, a staple that has shaped the country's diet since its introduction in the late 16th century. Potatoes form the backbone of many classic dishes, lending their versatility and comforting texture to meals that warm the soul. One such dish is colcannon, a simple yet satisfying blend of mashed potatoes, cabbage or kale, and butter. Often served with a sprinkle of spring onions, colcannon is a beloved accompaniment to meats and fish, embodying the essence of Irish comfort food.

Another iconic dish featuring potatoes is boxty, a type of potato pancake with roots in the rural north of Ireland. Boxty combines grated raw potatoes with mashed potatoes, flour, and buttermilk to create a batter that is then fried until golden brown. This versatile dish can be served as a side or enjoyed on its own, with various toppings such as smoked salmon or a dollop of sour cream adding a touch of indulgence.

No exploration of Irish cuisine would be complete without mentioning the renowned Irish stew. Traditionally made with mutton or lamb, this hearty dish combines tender meat with root vegetables such as potatoes, carrots, and onions, all simmered together in a savory broth. The slow-cooking process allows the flavors to meld beautifully, resulting in a dish that is both nourishing and full of depth. Variations of the stew may include barley or herbs, showcasing the adaptability of this beloved national dish.

Seafood also plays a prominent role in Irish culinary traditions, reflecting the island's proximity to the Atlantic Ocean. Fresh, locally sourced fish and shellfish are celebrated in dishes like Dublin Bay prawns, known for their sweet flavor and delicate texture. Served simply with garlic butter or featured in a creamy seafood chowder, these prawns exemplify the quality of Ireland's coastal bounty.

For those with a sweet tooth, traditional Irish desserts offer a delectable way to conclude a meal. One such treat is the barmbrack, a fruit-studded bread often enjoyed with a cup of tea. Traditionally associated with Halloween, barmbrack is known for the small trinkets baked inside, each with its own symbolic meaning. This ritual adds an element of fun and mystery to the enjoyment of this sweet bread.

Another beloved dessert is the Irish apple cake, a moist and flavorful treat that highlights the natural sweetness of apples. Often spiced with cinnamon and nutmeg, the cake is typically served warm, with a generous dollop of custard or cream, providing a comforting and satisfying end to a meal.

Soda bread is a quintessential element of Irish dining, its distinctive flavor and texture the result of using baking soda as a leavening agent. Made with simple ingredients such as flour, salt, and buttermilk, soda bread is a versatile accompaniment to both sweet and savory dishes. Whether served alongside a bowl of soup or spread with butter and jam, it remains a beloved staple in Irish households.

Irish cuisine also boasts a rich tradition of preserving and curing meats, with black pudding being a prime example. Made from pork blood, fat, and oatmeal, black pudding is a flavorful sausage often served as part of the traditional Irish breakfast. Its robust taste and satisfying texture make it a popular choice, whether enjoyed on its own or as a component of a larger meal.

The traditional Irish breakfast itself is a feast to behold, featuring a hearty combination of fried eggs, bacon, sausage, black and white pudding, baked beans, and grilled tomatoes. Often accompanied by slices of soda bread or toast, this substantial meal provides a delicious start to the day and fuels the body for the hours ahead.

For those interested in exploring these traditional dishes, there are several practical steps to take. Sourcing high-quality, locally produced ingredients can enhance the flavors and authenticity of your culinary creations. Farmers' markets and specialty food shops often offer a range of Irish products, from artisanal cheeses to freshly baked breads, providing a taste of Ireland's diverse agricultural offerings.

Experimenting with traditional recipes in your own kitchen can be a rewarding way to engage with Irish culture and heritage. Many classic dishes are simple to prepare, relying on straightforward techniques and readily available ingredients. Whether making a pot of stew or baking a loaf of soda bread, the process invites you to savor the experience and share the results with family and friends.

Attending cooking classes or workshops focused on Irish cuisine can deepen your understanding of traditional techniques and flavors. These experiences often provide hands-on instruction and insights into the cultural significance of each dish, enriching your appreciation for the culinary arts.

Traveling to Ireland offers the opportunity to experience traditional dishes in their native setting, with many restaurants and pubs serving authentic fare that showcases the island's culinary heritage. Sampling local specialties, whether in a bustling city or a quaint village, provides a delicious way to connect with the culture and people of Ireland.

Through its traditional dishes, Irish cuisine tells a story of resilience, resourcefulness, and community. Each meal is a celebration of the land and sea, a testament to the creativity and spirit of a people who have long cherished the simple pleasures of good food and company. By exploring these culinary traditions, you can embark on a flavorful journey that nourishes both body and soul, offering a taste of Ireland's past and present in every bite.

6.2 Modern Irish Cuisine

Modern Irish cuisine represents a dynamic fusion of tradition and innovation, reflecting the island's rich culinary heritage while embracing contemporary influences. Over the past few decades, Ireland has experienced a culinary renaissance, driven by a renewed appreciation for local, sustainable ingredients and a burgeoning community of talented chefs eager to explore new flavors and techniques. This evolution has transformed the perception of Irish food, highlighting its diversity and sophistication on the global stage.

The resurgence of interest in traditional ingredients has been a cornerstone of modern Irish cuisine. Chefs and home cooks alike have rediscovered the bounty of the land and sea, celebrating the natural flavors and quality of locally sourced produce. The emphasis on farm-to-table dining has fostered a closer connection between producers and consumers, with farmers' markets, artisanal food producers, and community-supported agriculture playing a vital role in the culinary landscape.

One of the defining characteristics of modern Irish cuisine is its emphasis on fresh, seasonal ingredients. The fertile soil and temperate climate of Ireland provide ideal conditions for growing a wide variety of fruits and vegetables, from earthy root vegetables to vibrant greens. These ingredients form the foundation of many contemporary dishes, offering a taste of Ireland's natural abundance.

Seafood, too, plays a prominent role in this culinary evolution. The island's expansive coastline yields an array of fresh fish and shellfish, from delicate salmon and trout to succulent oysters and mussels. Modern chefs have embraced these treasures from the sea, crafting dishes that highlight their natural flavors with minimal intervention. Light, flavorful preparations such as ceviche or grilled seafood platters showcase the purity and freshness of the catch.

The influence of global culinary trends has also left its mark on modern Irish cuisine. Chefs have drawn inspiration from international techniques and flavors, incorporating elements from Mediterranean, Asian, and other world cuisines into their repertoire. This cross-pollination of culinary ideas has resulted in innovative dishes that blend Irish ingredients with global influences, creating a unique and exciting dining experience.

A prime example of this fusion is the use of traditional Irish ingredients, such as black pudding or soda bread, in contemporary recipes. Black pudding, once a staple of the traditional Irish breakfast, has found new life as an ingredient in gourmet dishes, lending its rich, savory flavor to everything from salads to canapés. Similarly, soda bread, with its distinctive texture and taste, has been reimagined in a variety of forms, from artisanal loaves to creative desserts.

The rise of modern Irish cuisine has been propelled by a new generation of chefs who are pushing the boundaries of traditional cooking. These culinary innovators are committed to sustainability, sourcing their ingredients from local farms and producers to ensure freshness and support for the community. Their dedication to quality and creativity is evident in the dishes they craft, which often showcase the beauty and simplicity of Irish ingredients in unexpected ways.

Restaurants across Ireland are embracing this modern culinary ethos, offering menus that reflect the seasons and the stories of their ingredients. From bustling city bistros to serene countryside inns, these establishments provide a platform for chefs to express their creativity and passion for Irish food. Dining at one of these venues offers a glimpse into the future of Irish cuisine, where tradition and innovation coexist harmoniously.

For home cooks eager to explore modern Irish cuisine, there are several practical approaches to consider. Experimenting with fresh, local ingredients is a good starting point, allowing you to explore the flavors and textures that define Irish produce. Visiting farmers' markets or joining a community-supported agriculture program can provide access to high-quality ingredients while supporting local growers.

Incorporating global flavors and techniques into your cooking can also enhance your culinary repertoire. Exploring international cuisines and experimenting with spices, herbs, and cooking methods from around the world can inspire new interpretations of traditional Irish dishes. This approach encourages creativity and allows you to personalize recipes, infusing them with your own flair and taste preferences.

The growing interest in sustainable and ethical food practices has also influenced modern Irish cuisine, with many chefs and consumers prioritizing organic, locally sourced, and environmentally friendly options. Engaging with these practices can deepen your connection to the food you prepare and eat, fostering a greater appreciation for the journey from farm to table.

Cooking classes and workshops focused on modern Irish cuisine offer valuable opportunities to learn new techniques and gain insights into the evolving culinary landscape. These experiences provide hands-on instruction and guidance from experienced chefs, allowing you to develop your skills and confidence in the kitchen.

Traveling to Ireland to experience its culinary scene firsthand can be an unforgettable adventure. Exploring the diverse array of restaurants, cafes, and food festivals across the island offers a taste of modern Irish cuisine at its finest. Whether you're savoring a meal at a Michelin-starred restaurant or sampling street food at a local market, each bite reveals the creativity and passion that define Ireland's culinary renaissance.

In embracing modern Irish cuisine, you embark on a journey of discovery and exploration, where tradition meets innovation and the flavors of Ireland shine brightly. This ever-evolving culinary landscape invites you to celebrate the past while embracing the future, savoring each moment and each dish as a reflection of the island's vibrant spirit and rich heritage. Through the art of cooking and the joy of eating, modern Irish cuisine offers a feast for the senses, an invitation to explore, and a connection to the heart of Ireland.

6.3 Best Places to Eat

Ireland's culinary landscape is a vibrant tapestry of flavors, reflecting a rich history and a dynamic present. From traditional pubs to contemporary bistros, the country's dining scene offers something for every palate. Exploring the best places to eat in Ireland is not only a gastronomic adventure but also a journey through the island's diverse culture and heritage.

Dublin, the bustling capital, is a culinary hotspot that boasts an impressive array of dining options. At the heart of the city, you'll find Chapter One, a Michelin-starred restaurant known for its refined Irish cuisine. The menu celebrates seasonal ingredients and contemporary techniques, offering dishes that are as visually stunning as they are delicious. With a focus on local produce, Chapter One exemplifies the marriage of tradition and innovation that defines modern Irish dining.

For those seeking a more relaxed atmosphere, The Woollen Mills is a must-visit. This iconic eatery, housed in a historic building overlooking the River Liffey, serves up hearty, home-style dishes that pay homage to Irish culinary heritage. From its famous fish and chips to its delectable Guinness bread, The Woollen Mills offers a true taste of Dublin in a warm, welcoming setting.

Outside the capital, the culinary delights continue. In the picturesque town of Kinsale, often referred to as the "Gourmet Capital of Ireland," you'll find Fishy Fishy. As the name suggests, this seafood restaurant is renowned for its fresh, locally sourced catch. Nestled along the coast, Fishy Fishy offers diners the opportunity to savor dishes such as pan-seared scallops and monkfish curry, all while enjoying views of the harbor. The commitment to quality and sustainability is evident in every bite.

Galway, on Ireland's west coast, is another city where food lovers will find themselves spoiled for choice. One standout is Aniar, a Michelin-starred restaurant that takes a terroir-based approach to Irish cuisine. The menu is an ever-evolving celebration of the region's seasonal bounty, with dishes crafted from foraged ingredients and locally reared meats. Aniar's commitment to authenticity and innovation has earned it a reputation as a leader in Ireland's culinary renaissance.

For a more rustic experience, head to Moran's Oyster Cottage in Kilcolgan, County Galway. This charming establishment, set in a thatched cottage by the water's edge, has been serving oysters and seafood dishes for over 250 years. Whether you're indulging in a dozen oysters on the half shell or savoring a bowl of seafood chowder, Moran's offers an authentic taste of the sea in a setting steeped in history.

The culinary treasures of Ireland extend beyond its cities and towns. In the scenic County Clare, you'll find The Burren Smokehouse, where artisanal smoked salmon is the star of the show. This family-run business has been producing award-winning smoked fish for over three decades, using traditional smoking methods and the finest quality salmon. A visit to the smokehouse offers a chance to learn about the smoking process and sample the delicious results.

In Northern Ireland, Belfast has emerged as a culinary destination in its own right. The city is home to Ox, a Michelin-starred restaurant that emphasizes simplicity and seasonality in its dishes. The menu is a reflection of the changing seasons, with ingredients sourced from local farms and producers. Ox's commitment to sustainability and quality has made it a favorite among locals and visitors alike.

For a more casual dining experience, St. George's Market in Belfast is a vibrant hub of food and culture. This historic market, dating back to the 19th century, offers an array of food stalls serving everything from traditional Irish breakfasts to international cuisine. The lively atmosphere and diverse selection make it an ideal spot for foodies looking to sample a variety of flavors.

No exploration of Ireland's dining scene would be complete without a visit to one of its traditional pubs. The Brazen Head in Dublin, reputedly the oldest pub in Ireland, offers classic pub fare alongside a selection of craft beers and whiskeys.

With its cozy atmosphere and live music sessions, The Brazen Head provides an authentic taste of Irish hospitality and culture.

For those venturing to the scenic County Kerry, The Strawberry Field Pancake Cottage presents a delightful culinary detour. This quaint eatery, nestled in the heart of the countryside, specializes in both sweet and savory pancakes made with locally sourced ingredients. The charming setting and delicious offerings make it a favorite among locals and tourists alike.

When exploring the best places to eat in Ireland, it's essential to embrace the local customs and flavors. Whether dining in a Michelin-starred restaurant or enjoying a simple meal in a countryside cottage, each experience offers a unique glimpse into Ireland's culinary heritage. The emphasis on quality, sustainability, and local produce resonates throughout the country's dining establishments, ensuring that every meal is a celebration of the island's rich and diverse culture.

For travelers and food enthusiasts alike, Ireland's dining scene invites you to discover the stories behind each dish and the passion of those who create them. From the bustling streets of Dublin to the tranquil shores of Kinsale, the best places to eat in Ireland promise a journey of flavor, tradition, and innovation that will linger in your memory long after the meal is over.

6.4 Local Markets and Food Festivals

Local markets and food festivals in Ireland offer a vibrant and immersive experience, showcasing the island's rich culinary heritage and contemporary flavors. These gatherings are more than just venues for purchasing food; they are cultural celebrations that connect communities, highlight local producers, and invite visitors to engage with the authentic taste of Ireland. Attending these events provides an opportunity to explore the diverse range of Irish produce, meet the artisans behind the products, and participate in the lively atmosphere that defines Irish hospitality.

Farmers' markets have become a cornerstone of Ireland's food scene, embodying the farm-to-table ethos that has gained prominence in recent years. At these markets, local farmers and producers gather to sell fresh, seasonal produce directly to consumers. The emphasis on quality and sustainability is evident in the array of goods on offer, from organic vegetables and pasture-raised meats to artisanal cheeses and freshly baked breads. Each stall tells a story of dedication and passion, inviting you to taste the fruits of Irish soil and the labor of those who tend it.

Dublin's Temple Bar Food Market is a prime example of this thriving market culture. Located in the heart of the city, the market is a bustling hub of activity every Saturday, drawing both locals and tourists eager to sample the best of Irish produce. With its vibrant stalls and diverse offerings, the market showcases everything from handmade chocolates to craft beers, providing a feast for the senses and a chance to discover new flavors and culinary trends.

Beyond the capital, Cork's English Market stands as a testament to the enduring appeal of local markets in Ireland. Established in 1788, this historic market has long been a beloved institution, offering a wide selection of local and international foods. Visitors can savor the flavors of Cork through its famous spiced beef, artisanal cheeses, and freshly caught seafood. The market's lively atmosphere and friendly vendors create an inviting space where food lovers can indulge in the pleasures of browsing and tasting.

Food festivals, too, play a significant role in Ireland's culinary landscape, celebrating the island's unique flavors and bringing people together through shared appreciation of good food. These events often feature cooking demonstrations, tastings, and workshops, providing attendees with the chance to learn from renowned chefs and discover new culinary techniques.

One of the most celebrated food festivals in Ireland is the Galway International Oyster and Seafood Festival. Held annually in September, this event draws crowds from around the world to celebrate the bounty of the sea. Attendees can indulge in fresh oysters and seafood dishes while enjoying live music, entertainment, and the lively atmosphere that defines this iconic festival. The event also includes the prestigious World Oyster Opening Championship, adding an element of excitement and competition to the festivities.

In Northern Ireland, the Belfast Taste and Music Fest is a highlight of the culinary calendar. This festival combines the best of local food and music, offering a diverse program of events that cater to all tastes. Visitors can sample dishes from top restaurants, attend cooking demonstrations by celebrity chefs, and enjoy live performances by local musicians. The festival's inclusive and celebratory spirit provides a platform for showcasing Northern Ireland's burgeoning food scene.

The Listowel Food Fair in County Kerry is another noteworthy event, celebrating the rich agricultural heritage of the region. This fair offers a range of activities, from cook-offs and tastings to workshops and farm tours, providing a comprehensive exploration of the local food culture. The event encourages visitors to engage with the producers and learn about the origins of the food they enjoy, fostering a deeper connection to the land and the people who nurture it.

For those eager to explore the local markets and food festivals of Ireland, there are several practical steps to enhance the experience. Planning your visit around these events can provide a deeper insight into the local culture and culinary traditions. Checking the schedules and locations of markets and festivals in advance ensures that you can make the most of your time and not miss out on any must-see events.

Engaging with vendors and producers at these gatherings offers valuable opportunities to learn about the products and the passion that goes into their creation. Asking questions, sampling products, and taking the time to chat with the artisans can enrich your understanding of the local food scene and provide inspiration for your own culinary endeavors.

Participating in workshops and demonstrations is another way to deepen your appreciation for Irish cuisine. These sessions often provide hands-on experiences and expert insights, allowing you to develop new skills and discover innovative ways to incorporate Irish ingredients into your cooking.

For those interested in bringing a taste of Ireland home, many markets and festivals offer unique products that make for perfect souvenirs or gifts. From locally produced jams and chutneys to handmade crafts and textiles, these items capture the essence of Ireland and serve as lasting reminders of your culinary journey.

Exploring local markets and food festivals in Ireland is a feast for the senses, offering a window into the island's rich gastronomic heritage and vibrant present. Through these gatherings, you can taste the diversity of Irish produce, meet the passionate people behind the food, and experience the warmth and hospitality that define Irish culture. Whether you're savoring a freshly shucked oyster at a festival or browsing the stalls of a bustling market, each moment invites you to connect with the flavors and stories that make Ireland's culinary landscape so unique and captivating.

6.5 Whiskey and Brewery Tours

Whiskey and brewery tours in Ireland offer an intoxicating journey into the heart of the island's rich tradition of distilling and brewing, where centuries-old practices meet modern innovation. These tours provide a unique opportunity to explore the craftsmanship behind some of the world's most celebrated spirits and beers, offering a deeper appreciation for the flavors and stories that have shaped Ireland's liquid heritage.

The allure of Irish whiskey is undeniable, with its smooth, triple-distilled character setting it apart from its global counterparts. A visit to one of Ireland's historic distilleries offers an immersive experience that delves into the meticulous process of whiskey-making, from malting and mashing to fermentation and aging. The Jameson Distillery Bow St. in Dublin is a prime destination for whiskey enthusiasts. Stepping inside, you are transported to a world where tradition meets taste, with guided tours taking you through the storied history of Jameson whiskey. Visitors can witness the craftsmanship that goes into each bottle, concluding with a tasting that highlights the rich, complex flavors of this iconic spirit.

Beyond Dublin, the Midleton Distillery in County Cork offers another captivating whiskey experience. As the home of renowned brands such as Jameson, Redbreast, and Green Spot, Midleton provides a comprehensive tour that explores the art and science of whiskey production. The distillery's Heritage Centre offers interactive exhibits and displays that bring the history of Irish whiskey to life, making it an informative and engaging visit for both novice and seasoned whiskey aficionados.

For those seeking a more boutique experience, the Dingle Distillery in County Kerry offers a glimpse into the craft whiskey movement that is gaining momentum across Ireland. This independent distillery prides itself on producing small-batch, artisanal spirits that reflect the unique terroir of the region. A tour of the Dingle Distillery provides an intimate look at the passion and dedication that fuels the craft whiskey industry, with tastings that showcase the distinct character of their offerings.

In addition to whiskey, Ireland boasts a vibrant beer culture, with a growing number of craft breweries adding to the tapestry of traditional brewing practices. The Guinness Storehouse in Dublin is an iconic destination for beer lovers, offering an interactive and immersive experience that celebrates the legacy of Ireland's most famous stout. Visitors can explore the seven-story museum, which chronicles the history of Guinness from its founding in 1759 to its status as a global brand. The tour culminates in the Gravity Bar, where guests can enjoy a perfectly poured pint of Guinness while taking in panoramic views of Dublin.

For those interested in exploring the craft beer scene, a visit to Galway Bay Brewery offers an exciting introduction to Ireland's burgeoning craft beer movement. With a commitment to quality and innovation, Galway Bay Brewery produces a diverse range of beers that appeal to a wide variety of tastes. A tour of the brewery provides insight into the brewing process and the creative vision behind each brew, with tastings that highlight the bold flavors and innovative styles that define the craft beer experience.

In Northern Ireland, the Hilden Brewery in Lisburn stands as one of the oldest independent breweries on the island. This family-run establishment offers guided tours that explore the traditional brewing methods used to create their range of handcrafted ales and lagers. Guests can enjoy tastings in the brewery's taproom, where the warm and welcoming atmosphere invites conversation and camaraderie among beer enthusiasts.

For those planning a whiskey or brewery tour, there are several practical tips to enhance the experience. Researching the history and significance of each distillery or brewery can provide valuable context and deepen your appreciation for the craft. Understanding the nuances of whiskey and beer production, from the selection of ingredients to the aging process, can enrich your tour and provide a greater understanding of the complexities involved in creating these beloved beverages.

When visiting distilleries and breweries, taking advantage of guided tours and tastings allows you to engage with knowledgeable staff who can share insights and answer questions. These interactions offer an opportunity to learn about the unique characteristics of each product, from the flavor profiles of different whiskeys to the brewing techniques used to create distinctive beers.

Sampling a variety of products during tastings is also an essential part of the experience. Whether savoring the smooth notes of a single malt or the hoppy aroma of a craft IPA, each sip provides a sensory journey that reflects the artistry and dedication of the producers. Keeping an open mind and palate can lead to the discovery of new favorites and a deeper appreciation for the diversity of Irish spirits and beers.

Exploring the local culture and history surrounding each distillery and brewery can further enhance your tour. Many of these establishments are located in picturesque settings that offer opportunities for sightseeing and exploration. From the bustling streets of Dublin to the rugged beauty of the Wild Atlantic Way, Ireland's landscapes provide a stunning backdrop for your whiskey and brewery adventures.

Bringing home a bottle or two as a memento of your tour can serve as a lasting reminder of your experience. Whether it's a limited-edition whiskey or a selection of craft beers, these souvenirs offer a taste of Ireland that can be savored long after your visit.

Whiskey and brewery tours in Ireland offer a captivating journey through the island's rich tradition of distilling and brewing. Each tour provides a unique insight into the craftsmanship and passion that define Irish spirits and beers, inviting you to explore the flavors and stories that make these beverages an integral part of Ireland's cultural heritage. Whether you're a whiskey connoisseur or a craft beer enthusiast, these tours promise an unforgettable experience that will deepen your appreciation for the art of Irish drink-making.

CHAPTER 7: EXPLORING IRELAND'S REGIONS

7.1 The Charm of Galway

Galway, a spirited city on Ireland's west coast, enchants with its unique blend of history, culture, and natural beauty. Often referred to as the "City of Tribes," Galway's vibrant atmosphere and rich heritage make it a destination that captures the hearts of visitors and locals alike. With its colorful streets, lively arts scene, and stunning coastal landscapes, Galway offers a tapestry of experiences that invite exploration and discovery.

The city's history is woven into its very fabric, with medieval remnants standing alongside modern developments. Strolling through the cobbled streets of the Latin Quarter, you'll encounter historic landmarks such as the Spanish Arch, which dates back to the 16th century. This area, once a bustling trading hub, now thrives as a cultural center, filled with bustling cafes, shops, and galleries that showcase the creativity and spirit of Galway.

Galway's charm extends beyond its architecture. The city's vibrant arts scene is a testament to its status as a cultural capital. The Galway International Arts Festival, held annually in July, is a highlight of the cultural calendar, attracting artists and performers from around the world. The festival transforms the city into a vibrant stage, with theater, music, and visual arts performances that captivate audiences and celebrate the diversity of human expression.

Music is an integral part of life in Galway, infusing the city with a melodic energy that resonates from street corners to lively pubs. Traditional Irish music sessions, known as "seisiúns," are a common sight in Galway's many pubs, where local musicians gather to share tunes and stories. Venues like The Crane Bar and Tig Coili are famed for their live music, offering an authentic taste of Ireland's rich musical heritage.

The sound of fiddles, flutes, and bodhráns create an irresistible rhythm that invites visitors to tap their feet and join in the celebration.

For those seeking to explore Galway's culinary offerings, the city's food scene is a delightful fusion of tradition and innovation. Galway's proximity to the Atlantic Ocean ensures an abundance of fresh seafood, with oysters being a particular specialty. The Galway Oyster Festival, held each September, celebrates this delicacy with tastings, competitions, and live entertainment. Local restaurants such as Ard Bia at Nimmos and Kai Café & Restaurant offer menus that highlight seasonal, locally sourced ingredients, providing a taste of the region's natural bounty.

Galway's coastal location also offers an array of outdoor adventures for nature enthusiasts. The Wild Atlantic Way, a scenic coastal route, invites exploration of the rugged landscapes and breathtaking vistas that define Ireland's west coast. A short drive from the city, Connemara National Park beckons with its dramatic mountain ranges, serene lakes, and diverse wildlife. Hiking trails wind through the park, offering opportunities to immerse yourself in the beauty and tranquility of the Irish countryside.

The Aran Islands, located just off the coast of Galway, are another must-visit destination for those seeking to experience the region's natural wonders. A ferry ride from the mainland transports you to a world where time seems to stand still. The islands are renowned for their stunning limestone landscapes, ancient stone forts, and traditional Irish culture. Exploring the islands by bike or on foot allows you to discover hidden coves, windswept cliffs, and the warmth of the local communities.

Galway's charm lies not only in its scenic beauty and cultural offerings but also in its welcoming and inclusive spirit. The city's residents, known for their friendliness and hospitality, create an inviting atmosphere that makes visitors feel at home. This sense of community is palpable during events such as the Galway Races, a week-long festival of horse racing and celebration that draws crowds from near and far. The event is a vibrant showcase of Irish culture, with fashion, entertainment, and camaraderie taking center stage.

For those interested in delving deeper into Galway's history, a visit to the Galway City Museum provides a comprehensive look at the city's past and present. The museum's exhibits explore the region's archaeology, history, and culture, offering insights into the events and people that have shaped Galway over the centuries. From prehistoric artifacts to contemporary art, the museum provides a fascinating journey through time.

As the sun sets over Galway Bay, the city takes on a new allure, with its streets and waterfront glowing in the evening light. A stroll along the Salthill Promenade offers a chance to savor the tranquility of the sea and the beauty of the horizon. The gentle crash of waves provides a soothing soundtrack, inviting reflection and relaxation.

Galway's charm is a harmonious blend of tradition and modernity, where history and culture converge to create a destination that is both timeless and dynamic. Whether you're exploring its historic streets, savoring its culinary delights, or immersing yourself in its vibrant arts scene, Galway offers an experience that lingers long after your visit has ended. It's a city that invites you to embrace its spirit, celebrate its culture, and discover the magic that makes it one of Ireland's most enchanting places.

7.2 The Beauty of Cork and Kerry

Cork and Kerry, two gems of Ireland's southwestern region, boast a stunning blend of natural beauty, rich history, and vibrant culture. Known for their dramatic coastlines, lush landscapes, and charming towns, these counties offer a captivating experience that draws visitors from around the world. From the bustling city of Cork to the serene beauty of the Ring of Kerry, this region invites exploration and discovery at every turn.

Cork, often referred to as the "Rebel County," is a lively city steeped in history and character. Its streets are lined with colorful buildings and lively markets, offering a warm welcome to all who visit. The English Market, a culinary landmark in the heart of the city, is a must-visit destination for food lovers. With its wide array of local produce, artisanal goods, and international delicacies, the market provides a feast for the senses and a chance to experience the flavors of Cork.

The city is also home to a thriving arts scene, with galleries, theaters, and music venues that showcase the creativity and talent of the region. St. Fin Barre's Cathedral, a stunning example of Gothic Revival architecture, stands as a testament to Cork's rich history. Its intricate carvings and stained glass windows offer a glimpse into the artistic heritage of the city.

Beyond the city limits, County Cork's landscapes unfold into a tapestry of rolling hills, rugged coastlines, and quaint villages. The Beara Peninsula, a hidden gem on the western edge of the county, offers breathtaking views and a serene escape from the bustle of everyday life. The peninsula is dotted with charming towns such as Castletownbere and Allihies, where visitors can immerse themselves in the tranquility of the Irish countryside.

Kinsale, a picturesque harbor town in County Cork, is renowned for its maritime history and culinary excellence. The town's colorful streets are lined with gourmet restaurants and traditional pubs, offering a taste of the region's rich culinary heritage. Kinsale's scenic harbor provides a backdrop for leisurely walks and water-based activities, while its historic sites, such as Charles Fort, invite exploration of the town's storied past.

Traveling westward, the county of Kerry enchants with its awe-inspiring landscapes and charming towns. The Ring of Kerry, a scenic drive that loops around the Iveragh Peninsula, is one of the most iconic routes in Ireland. With its rugged coastline, majestic mountains, and shimmering lakes, the Ring of Kerry offers a visual feast that captures the essence of Ireland's natural beauty.

The town of Killarney, nestled at the heart of Kerry, serves as a gateway to this stunning region. Killarney National Park, with its lush woodlands, sparkling lakes, and historic landmarks, offers a haven for outdoor enthusiasts and nature lovers. The park is home to Muckross House, an elegant Victorian mansion surrounded by manicured gardens and scenic trails. Visitors can explore the house's opulent interiors and learn about its fascinating history, or simply enjoy a leisurely stroll through the park's serene landscapes.

The Dingle Peninsula, another highlight of County Kerry, is a place where time seems to stand still. The peninsula's dramatic cliffs, sandy beaches, and ancient ruins create a landscape that is both rugged and enchanting. The town of Dingle, with its lively atmosphere and friendly locals, offers a warm welcome to all who visit. Dingle's vibrant arts scene, traditional music sessions, and delicious seafood make it a destination that delights the senses and nourishes the soul.

For those seeking adventure, the Skellig Islands, located off the coast of Kerry, offer a unique and unforgettable experience. Skellig Michael, a UNESCO World Heritage Site, is home to an ancient monastic settlement perched atop steep cliffs. The island's remote location and dramatic scenery create an otherworldly atmosphere that has captivated visitors for centuries. A boat trip to the Skellig Islands provides an opportunity to explore this remarkable site and witness the rich biodiversity that thrives in its waters.

Throughout Cork and Kerry, the warmth and hospitality of the local communities create an inviting atmosphere that makes visitors feel at home. The region's cultural heritage is celebrated through festivals, events, and traditional practices that offer a glimpse into the heart of Irish life. Whether it's the lively music sessions of Dingle, the culinary delights of Kinsale, or the scenic beauty of the Ring of Kerry, each experience invites visitors to connect with the spirit of the land and the people who call it home.

Cork and Kerry, with their breathtaking landscapes, rich history, and vibrant culture, offer a journey of discovery that lingers long after the visit has ended. From the bustling streets of Cork to the serene beauty of Kerry's coastal routes, this region invites exploration and celebration of the natural and cultural treasures that define Ireland's southwestern corner. Whether you're wandering through the English Market, exploring the ancient ruins of Skellig Michael, or simply savoring the stunning views along the Ring of Kerry, the beauty of Cork and Kerry promises an unforgettable experience that captures the heart and soul of Ireland.

7.3 Northern Ireland's Rich Heritage

Northern Ireland, a land rich in history and cultural heritage, offers a captivating journey through time for those eager to explore its diverse landscape and storied past. From ancient archaeological sites to the echoes of more recent historical events, Northern Ireland invites visitors to delve into its multifaceted identity. This region, with its stunning natural beauty and vibrant cities, serves as a living testament to the resilience and spirit of its people.

One cannot discuss Northern Ireland's heritage without mentioning the iconic Giant's Causeway. This UNESCO World Heritage site, located on the north coast, is a geological wonder that has fascinated visitors for centuries. Comprising approximately 40,000 interlocking basalt columns, the

Causeway was formed by volcanic activity around 60 million years ago. The natural phenomenon is steeped in legend, with stories of the giant Finn McCool who, according to folklore, built the causeway to confront his Scottish rival. Walking along the hexagonal stones, one can almost hear the whispers of ancient tales carried by the sea breeze.

Not far from the Causeway lies the historic city of Derry, also known as Londonderry. A visit to Derry offers an opportunity to explore one of the best-preserved walled cities in Europe. The 17th-century city walls encircle a vibrant center, providing a tangible link to the past and a stunning vantage point from which to view the cityscape. Derry's history is marked by significant events, including the Siege of Derry in 1689 and the civil rights marches of the 20th century. The Museum of Free Derry offers valuable insights into the city's more recent history, focusing on the period known as The Troubles. Through personal stories and artifacts, the museum provides a moving account of the struggle for civil rights and the quest for peace.

Belfast, the capital of Northern Ireland, is a city that has reinvented itself while honoring its rich industrial heritage. Known as the birthplace of the Titanic, Belfast offers visitors a chance to explore the city's shipbuilding past at the Titanic Belfast museum. Housed in a striking building that evokes the spirit of the ill-fated ship, the museum guides visitors through the Titanic's conception, construction, and tragic maiden voyage. The interactive exhibits and immersive experiences provide a poignant reminder of the human stories behind the ship's legacy.

The Ulster Folk Museum, located just outside Belfast, offers another glimpse into Northern Ireland's past. This open-air museum recreates rural and urban life from the early 20th century, with reconstructed buildings, traditional crafts, and costumed guides bringing history to life. Visitors can wander through the village streets, explore the working farm, and engage with demonstrations that showcase traditional skills such as basket weaving and blacksmithing. The museum provides a unique opportunity to experience the everyday lives of Northern Ireland's ancestors and gain a deeper understanding of the cultural traditions that continue to shape the region.

For those interested in ancient history, the Navan Fort in County Armagh is a must-visit site. This ancient ceremonial complex, dating back to the Iron Age, is steeped in myth and legend. Believed to be the ancient capital of Ulster and the seat of the legendary King Conchobar mac Nessa, Navan Fort offers a fascinating insight into the rituals and beliefs of Ireland's early inhabitants. The nearby Navan Centre provides interactive exhibits and archaeological displays that delve into the site's history and significance, offering a comprehensive exploration of Northern Ireland's ancient past.

Northern Ireland's natural landscapes are as much a part of its heritage as its historical sites. The Mourne Mountains, a range of granite peaks in County Down, have inspired writers and artists for generations. With their rugged beauty and sweeping vistas, the Mournes offer a haven for outdoor enthusiasts and a source of inspiration for those seeking to connect with nature. The mountains are crisscrossed with trails that invite exploration, providing opportunities for hiking, climbing, and simply taking in the breathtaking scenery.

The Glens of Antrim, a series of nine picturesque valleys, offer another glimpse of Northern Ireland's natural heritage. Each glen has its own unique character, with lush forests, cascading waterfalls, and charming villages that invite exploration. The glens are steeped in folklore, with tales of fairies, giants, and ancient warriors woven into the landscape. A drive along the Antrim Coast Road offers stunning views of the glens and the rugged coastline, providing a scenic journey through one of Northern Ireland's most enchanting regions.

Throughout Northern Ireland, festivals and events celebrate the region's cultural heritage, offering a chance to engage with local traditions and customs. The Foyle Maritime Festival in Derry, for example, celebrates the city's maritime history with a vibrant program of events, including boat races, music performances, and cultural activities. The Belfast International Arts Festival brings together artists from around the world, showcasing a diverse array of performances and exhibitions that highlight the region's creative spirit.

Northern Ireland's rich heritage is a tapestry of history, culture, and natural beauty, offering a journey of discovery for those who venture to its shores. From the ancient stones of the Giant's Causeway to the vibrant streets of Belfast, each experience invites exploration and reflection on the stories that have shaped this remarkable region. Whether you're delving into the myths of Navan Fort, wandering through the glens of Antrim, or connecting with the spirit of Derry's past, Northern Ireland promises an unforgettable journey into the heart of its heritage.

7.4 The Midlands and Ancient East

Ireland's Midlands and Ancient East, often overshadowed by the more famous coastal regions, hold a wealth of history and cultural heritage that beckon exploration. This area serves as a living tapestry, weaving together ancient monuments, medieval castles, and charming villages that tell the story of Ireland's past. From the prehistoric sites that whisper tales of ancient rituals to bustling market towns that reflect centuries of trade and community, the Midlands and Ancient East offer a captivating glimpse into a world where history is a constant companion.

The Midlands region is characterized by its lush greenery, rolling hills, and tranquil lakes, providing a serene backdrop for the many historical treasures that dot the landscape. One of the most intriguing sites is the Hill of Tara in County Meath, an ancient ceremonial complex that was once the seat of the High Kings of Ireland. This mystical site, with its panoramic views and enigmatic mounds, offers a connection to Ireland's distant past. Standing on the Hill of Tara, one can almost feel the echoes of ancient gatherings and rituals, a reminder of the enduring significance of this sacred place.

Not far from Tara, the Brú na Bóinne complex, a UNESCO World Heritage site, is home to some of the most impressive megalithic tombs in Europe. Newgrange, the most famous of these, dates back over 5,000 years and predates both Stonehenge and the Great Pyramids of Giza. The passage tomb, with its intricately carved stones and precisely aligned entrance, is a testament to the advanced knowledge and skills of its builders. Visiting Newgrange offers a rare opportunity to step inside a structure that has stood the test of time, providing a tangible link to the ancient peoples who once inhabited the region.

The Midlands are also home to numerous medieval castles and monastic sites that reflect the region's rich history. Birr Castle in County Offaly, for example, combines historical significance with scientific innovation. The castle's grounds house the Great Telescope, once the largest in the world, a symbol of the 19th-century scientific advancements that took place in this rural setting. Visitors to Birr Castle can explore the beautifully landscaped gardens and the fascinating science center, offering a unique blend of history and discovery.

Clonmacnoise, an ancient monastic site located on the banks of the River Shannon, is another highlight of the Midlands. Founded in the 6th century, Clonmacnoise was a major center of religion, learning, and trade throughout the medieval period. Today, its atmospheric ruins, including round towers, high crosses, and churches, invite contemplation and reflection on the spiritual and cultural legacy of this once-thriving community.

Moving eastward, the Ancient East region of Ireland is a treasure trove of historical and cultural sites that span millennia. The Rock of Cashel in County Tipperary is one of the most iconic landmarks in the area. Perched on a limestone hill, this medieval fortress complex was once the seat of the kings of Munster and later a significant ecclesiastical center. The site's impressive collection of buildings, including a round tower, a cathedral, and a chapel, offers a captivating glimpse into Ireland's medieval past.

Kilkenny, a city renowned for its medieval architecture and vibrant arts scene, is a must-visit destination in the Ancient East. Kilkenny Castle, a stunning example of Norman architecture, stands proudly along the River Nore, its imposing presence a reminder of the city's storied past. Visitors can explore the castle's opulent interiors and stroll through its beautifully maintained gardens. The city's narrow streets, lined with historic buildings, are home to a thriving community of artisans and craftspeople, making Kilkenny a hub of creativity and culture.

Further east, the Wicklow Mountains provide a dramatic natural setting for some of the region's most significant historical sites. Glendalough, a glacial valley with a rich monastic heritage, is renowned for its stunning landscapes and ancient ruins. Founded by St. Kevin in the 6th century, Glendalough became a center of pilgrimage and learning, attracting scholars and monks from across Europe. The site, with its serene lakes and forested hills, offers a peaceful retreat and a chance to connect with Ireland's spiritual heritage.

Throughout the Midlands and Ancient East, the landscape is dotted with charming villages and market towns that offer a warm welcome to visitors. These communities, with their traditional pubs, local festivals, and vibrant markets, provide a glimpse into the everyday lives of the people who call this region home. Engaging with the local culture, whether through a lively music session in a pub or a visit to a bustling farmers' market, adds depth and richness to the experience of exploring this captivating area.

For those interested in delving deeper into the region's history, several heritage trails and guided tours offer structured opportunities to discover the hidden gems and lesser-known sites of the Midlands and Ancient East. These experiences provide valuable insights into the region's past, highlighting the stories and traditions that have shaped its identity.

Ireland's Midlands and Ancient East, with their wealth of historical and cultural treasures, offer a journey of discovery that invites exploration and reflection. From the ancient mounds of the Hill of Tara to the medieval splendor of Kilkenny Castle, each site tells a story that adds to the rich tapestry of Ireland's heritage. Whether you're wandering through the atmospheric ruins of Clonmacnoise or savoring the warmth of a traditional village, the Midlands and Ancient East promise a journey that lingers in the memory and captures the heart.

7.5 The Undiscovered West

The western coast of Ireland, often overshadowed by its more famous counterparts, holds a treasure trove of hidden gems waiting to be uncovered by the intrepid traveler. This region, known for its rugged beauty and untamed landscapes, offers a captivating blend of natural wonders, historic sites, and authentic cultural experiences that reflect the heart and soul of Ireland. From the dramatic cliffs and serene beaches to the charming towns and ancient ruins, the undiscovered West invites exploration and discovery.

Connemara, a region renowned for its wild landscapes and remote beauty, epitomizes the allure of the West. Sweeping boglands, shimmering lakes, and the majestic Twelve Bens mountain range create a dramatic backdrop that captivates the senses. The area is a haven for outdoor enthusiasts, offering countless opportunities for hiking, cycling, and horseback riding. The Connemara National Park, with its network of trails and panoramic vistas, provides a perfect introduction to the region's natural splendor. As you traverse the landscape, the ever-changing light and weather paint an ever-evolving canvas that inspires awe and wonder.

Nestled within Connemara is the picturesque village of Roundstone. Known for its vibrant arts scene and traditional music, Roundstone offers a glimpse into the creative spirit of the West. The village's harbor, dotted with colorful fishing boats, provides a tranquil setting for leisurely strolls and reflection. Local artisans, inspired by the surrounding beauty, produce a range of unique crafts and artworks that capture the essence of the region. Visiting Roundstone offers an opportunity to connect with the local community and experience the warmth and hospitality for which the West is renowned.

Further south, the Burren in County Clare presents a landscape that is both haunting and beautiful. This karst limestone region, known for its unique geology and rich biodiversity, offers a stark contrast to the lush greenery typically associated with Ireland. The Burren's rocky terrain is home to an array of rare plant species, including colorful orchids and alpine flowers, which thrive in the cracks and crevices of the limestone. Walking through this otherworldly landscape, one can discover ancient tombs, ring forts, and stone walls that speak of the region's long and storied history.

The Cliffs of Moher, located at the southwestern edge of the Burren, are one of Ireland's most iconic natural landmarks. Rising over 200 meters above the Atlantic Ocean, the cliffs offer breathtaking views that stretch as far as the Aran Islands and beyond. The visitor center provides insights into the geology and wildlife of the area, while the cliffside paths invite exploration and appreciation of the stunning vistas. As the waves crash against the cliffs below, the sheer scale and beauty of the landscape instill a sense of awe and reverence for the natural world.

The town of Westport in County Mayo, with its Georgian architecture and lively atmosphere, serves as a gateway to the many wonders of the West. Westport's tree-lined streets and colorful shopfronts create a welcoming and vibrant environment, while its bustling pubs and restaurants offer a taste of the region's culinary delights. The town is an ideal base for exploring nearby attractions such as Croagh Patrick, Ireland's holy mountain, and Clew Bay, with its myriad of islands and stunning coastal scenery.

A journey along the Wild Atlantic Way, a scenic coastal route that stretches from Donegal to Cork, offers a chance to discover some of the West's hidden treasures. This route, with its dramatic seascapes and charming coastal villages, provides a captivating introduction to the region's diverse landscapes and rich cultural heritage. The journey invites travelers to immerse themselves in the sights, sounds, and flavors of the West, from the rugged cliffs and pristine beaches to the traditional music and warm hospitality of the local communities.

For those seeking an authentic cultural experience, the Gaeltacht regions of the West offer a unique opportunity to engage with Ireland's linguistic and cultural heritage. These areas, where Irish is the primary language, provide a glimpse into a way of life that has been preserved for generations. Visitors can participate in traditional music sessions, storytelling events, and cultural festivals that celebrate the rich traditions of the region. The warmth and generosity of the local people create an inviting atmosphere that encourages connection and understanding.

The undiscovered West, with its breathtaking landscapes, rich history, and vibrant culture, offers a journey of discovery that promises to linger in the memory long after the visit has ended. From the wild beauty of Connemara to the dramatic cliffs of Moher, each experience invites exploration and reflection on the stories and traditions that have shaped this remarkable region. Whether you're wandering through the rocky terrain of the Burren, savoring the flavors of Westport, or connecting with the spirit of the Gaeltacht, the West promises an unforgettable journey into the heart of Ireland's natural and cultural heritage.

7.6 Regional Itineraries and Highlights

Embarking on a journey through Ireland unveils a tapestry of landscapes and stories that have shaped its regions, each offering a unique glimpse into the heart of the Emerald Isle. Crafting regional itineraries allows travelers to dive deep into the diverse offerings of each area, ensuring an enriching experience that encompasses history, culture, and natural beauty. Below, we'll traverse some of Ireland's most captivating regions, highlighting must-see sights and hidden gems along the way.

Starting in the enchanting east, Dublin serves as the pulsating heart of Ireland. The city's vibrant energy is palpable, with its cobbled streets and historic landmarks inviting exploration. A stroll along the River Liffey leads to the iconic Ha'penny Bridge, a symbol of Dublin's charm. Trinity College, home to the ancient Book of Kells, offers a window into Ireland's scholarly past. As the day wanes, Temple Bar's lively atmosphere beckons with its myriad pubs and the resonating sounds of traditional Irish music.

Venturing south from Dublin, the medieval city of Kilkenny is a treasure trove of history and craftsmanship. Kilkenny Castle, with its imposing facade and lush gardens, stands as a testament to Norman influence. The city's narrow lanes are dotted with artisan workshops, where craftspeople continue age-old traditions in pottery and design. Nearby, the scenic beauty of the Wicklow Mountains National Park offers trails that weave through heather-covered hills and serene glacial valleys.

In the heart of Ireland, the Midlands offer a tranquil escape with their rolling landscapes and historical sites. The ancient monastic settlement of Clonmacnoise, perched on the banks of the River Shannon, whispers stories of spiritual and scholarly pursuits. Its round towers and high crosses stand silent yet powerful, echoing the religious significance of the past. For a taste of local life, Athlone's bustling markets and cozy pubs provide a warm welcome.

Turning to the west, the rugged beauty of County Clare captivates with its dramatic cliffs and unique karst landscapes. The Cliffs of Moher, towering majestically over the Atlantic Ocean, offer vistas that inspire awe and introspection. The Burren, a stark yet beautiful limestone plateau, invites exploration with its rare flora and ancient stone structures. Ennis, a town known for its traditional music, presents an opportunity to experience the soulful melodies that define Irish culture.

Further north, the mystical landscapes of County Sligo and County Donegal beckon with their untamed beauty. Sligo, immortalized in the poetry of W.B. Yeats, is a place where myth and reality intertwine. Benbulben Mountain, with its distinctive table-top shape, looms over the landscape, inviting hikers to explore its rugged trails. Donegal, with its pristine beaches and towering sea cliffs, is a haven for those seeking solitude and natural splendor. The Slieve League cliffs, among the highest in Europe, offer breathtaking views that stretch to the horizon.

On the southern coast, the counties of Cork and Kerry offer a blend of vibrant cities and serene landscapes. Cork City pulsates with life, its markets and festivals reflecting a rich cultural tapestry. Kinsale, with its picturesque harbor and gourmet offerings, is a culinary delight. The Ring of Kerry, a scenic drive that loops around the Iveragh Peninsula, presents dramatic coastlines and quaint villages that embody the spirit of the region. Killarney National Park, with its lakes and woodlands, is a sanctuary for wildlife and a paradise for outdoor enthusiasts.

The northern reaches of the island hold the intrigue of Northern Ireland, where history and natural beauty converge. Belfast, a city reborn, offers insights into its industrial past and cultural renaissance. The Titanic Belfast museum, with its innovative exhibits, tells the story of the ill-fated ship and the city's shipbuilding legacy. The Causeway Coast, with its stunning vistas and the iconic Giant's Causeway, is a natural wonder that captivates all who visit.

Ireland's regional itineraries offer a journey through a land where every turn reveals a story, a tradition, or a breathtaking view. Whether tracing the footsteps of ancient monks, marveling at geological wonders, or savoring the rhythms of traditional music, each experience adds depth to the tapestry of the Emerald Isle. These highlights and hidden gems invite travelers to forge their own paths, discovering the heart and soul of Ireland along the way.

7.7 Local Guides and Tours

Navigating the rich tapestry of Ireland's landscapes and history can be an overwhelming venture for any traveler. The allure of its ancient ruins, vibrant cities, and breathtaking coastlines is undeniable, yet to truly understand and appreciate the depths of this land, one might consider the invaluable insights offered by local guides and tours. These knowledgeable insiders not only bring the stories of Ireland to life but also provide access to hidden gems and unique experiences that might otherwise remain undiscovered.

Local guides are storytellers at heart, weaving narratives that breathe life into Ireland's past and present. Whether it's the lively streets of Dublin or the quiet hills of Connemara, these guides possess a deep-rooted connection to their homeland, infused with personal anecdotes and historical insights that enrich any exploration. A guided tour of Dublin, for instance, might take you through the cobbled streets of Temple Bar, where tales of literary giants such as James Joyce and Samuel Beckett intertwine with the vibrant energy of the city. With a guide leading the way, one can uncover the layers of history hidden within the facades of Georgian architecture or the whispers of rebellion and revolution along O'Connell Street.

In the heart of Ireland, the ancient monastic site of Glendalough offers a journey back in time. A local guide can illuminate the spiritual significance of this serene valley, sharing stories of St. Kevin and the monastic community that once thrived here. As you wander among the ruins, the guide's voice paints a picture of medieval life, from the daily rituals of the monks to the bustling activity of pilgrims who sought solace and learning within these sacred walls. The guide's expertise extends beyond historical facts, often incorporating local legends and folklore that add a layer of enchantment to the experience.

For those seeking adventure along Ireland's rugged coastline, local tours offer a gateway to the natural wonders that define the island's periphery. The Wild Atlantic Way, with its dramatic cliffs and sweeping vistas, is best experienced with a guide who knows the land intimately. From the towering Cliffs of Moher to the secluded beaches of Donegal, these guides provide not only logistical support but also a deeper understanding of the geological forces that shaped the landscape. Their knowledge of the flora and fauna, as well as the conservation efforts in place, enriches the journey and fosters a greater appreciation for the natural world.

The culinary landscape of Ireland, often overshadowed by its scenic beauty, is a delightful revelation for those willing to explore its local flavors. Guided food tours offer a taste of Ireland's evolving gastronomy, from traditional dishes to modern interpretations that showcase the island's rich agricultural heritage. In Cork, a city known for its food culture, a local guide can lead you through the bustling English Market, where artisanal cheeses, fresh seafood, and homemade breads tempt the senses. Along the way, the guide shares stories of local producers and the farm-to-table movement that is redefining Irish cuisine.

In Northern Ireland, the Causeway Coast presents an opportunity to explore a region steeped in myth and natural beauty. A guided tour of the Giant's Causeway, with its basalt columns and legendary tales of giants, offers a fascinating blend of geology and folklore. Local guides bring the story of Finn McCool to life, while also explaining the scientific processes that created this UNESCO World Heritage site. Nearby, the historic city of Derry, with its well-preserved walls and tumultuous past, is best explored with a guide who can navigate the complex history of the city from the Siege of Derry to The Troubles and beyond.

Beyond the well-trodden paths, local guides have the unique ability to unlock the secrets of hidden Ireland. In the lesser-known regions, such as the Slieve Bloom Mountains or the Arigna Mining Experience, guides offer insights into the lives of communities that have shaped Ireland's cultural landscape. Whether it's a walk through the untouched beauty of the Wicklow Mountains or a tour of the ancient passage tombs at Carrowkeel, these guides reveal the stories of resilience and ingenuity that define the Irish spirit.

For those interested in Ireland's vibrant arts scene, guided tours of galleries, studios, and performance spaces provide a window into the creative pulse of the country. In cities like Galway and Kilkenny, local guides can introduce travelers to the artists and craftspeople who continue to draw inspiration from Ireland's landscapes and traditions. These tours offer a chance to engage with the creative process, whether it's witnessing a potter at work or attending a traditional music session in a local pub.

Local guides and tours offer more than just convenience; they provide a connection to the soul of Ireland. Their knowledge and passion illuminate the paths less traveled, inviting travelers to engage with the land and its people in meaningful ways. Whether you're tracing the footsteps of ancient monks, savoring the flavors of a farm-to-table meal, or standing in awe of nature's grandeur, these guides ensure that your journey through Ireland is rich with discovery and understanding. Through their eyes, the Emerald Isle reveals its true essence, a place where history and culture converge in a tapestry of unforgettable experiences.

CHAPTER 8: CONCLUSION AND FURTHER RESOURCES

8.1 Reflecting on Your Journey

Stepping back from the whirlwind of travel, it's essential to pause and reflect on the journey just undertaken. Travel is not merely an act of moving from one location to another; it is an intricate dance of encounters and experiences that leave an indelible mark on the soul. As you sift through memories, photographs, and perhaps a few souvenirs, consider what this journey has taught you—not just about the places you visited, but about yourself and the world at large.

Recall the first steps you took on this adventure. There was likely a mix of excitement and apprehension, a feeling of stepping into the unknown. Each day presented new challenges and discoveries, whether navigating a bustling city or finding solitude in a remote landscape. Travel demands adaptability, urging you to step outside your comfort zone and embrace unfamiliar cultures and customs. These moments of adaptation are where growth occurs, where the traveler becomes a more seasoned observer of the world.

Think about the people you met along the way. Each interaction, whether brief or enduring, adds depth to the narrative of your journey. Perhaps it was a friendly local who offered directions or shared a story, or fellow travelers whose paths intersected with yours, creating shared memories. These connections remind us of our shared humanity, transcending language and cultural barriers. Reflecting on these interactions, consider how they have broadened your perspective, offering new insights into lives lived differently from your own.

The landscapes and landmarks visited also play a crucial role in shaping your journey. Standing before natural wonders or historical sites often evokes a sense of awe and wonderment. These places, steeped in history and beauty, speak to the enduring legacy of the world we inhabit. Whether it was the vast expanse of a mountain range, the intricate architecture of a centuries-old cathedral, or the quiet beauty of a hidden cove, each location contributed to the tapestry of your travel experience.

Consider the lessons learned from navigating the logistical aspects of travel. From planning itineraries to managing budgets, travel requires a degree of organization and foresight. Reflecting on these challenges, you might recognize newfound skills or areas for improvement. The ability to adapt plans when faced with unforeseen circumstances is a valuable takeaway, teaching resilience and resourcefulness in the face of change.

As you reflect, think about the moments that took you by surprise. Travel often presents unexpected encounters or events that leave a lasting impression. These surprises, whether serendipitous meetings, spontaneous adventures, or even minor misadventures, add an element of unpredictability and excitement to the journey. They remind us that travel is as much about the journey itself as it is about the destination, urging us to embrace the unexpected with an open heart.

Journaling or documenting your experiences can be a powerful tool in the reflection process. Writing down thoughts, feelings, and observations allows you to process and internalize the journey more fully. This practice not only preserves memories but also provides an opportunity to revisit and relive the adventure long after it has concluded. Looking back through these reflections, you may notice changes in your perspectives, shifts in your understanding of the places visited, and growth in your personal outlook.

Reflecting on the sensory experiences of travel adds another layer to your journey. The flavors of local cuisine, the sounds of bustling markets or tranquil nature, and the vibrant colors of foreign landscapes all contribute to the richness of travel. These sensory memories evoke powerful emotions and can transport you back to specific moments in time. Consider how these experiences have influenced your appreciation for diversity and cultural expression.

The end of a journey often brings a mix of emotions—satisfaction, nostalgia, and perhaps a hint of longing for more. As you return to the rhythms of everyday life, the challenge lies in integrating the lessons and experiences gained from travel into your daily existence. This integration might manifest as a renewed appreciation for your surroundings, a commitment to embracing new challenges, or a desire to continue exploring the world.

Finally, consider the impact of your journey on the places and communities you visited. Responsible travel involves being mindful of the environmental and cultural footprint left behind. Reflect on how you interacted with local communities and the efforts made to support sustainable practices. This awareness fosters a deeper connection to the places visited and encourages a commitment to preserving their beauty for future generations.

Reflecting on your journey is an essential component of travel, allowing you to distill the essence of your experiences and carry them forward into your life. Each journey, with its unique blend of challenges and joys, contributes to your personal growth and understanding of the world. As you reflect, embrace the memories formed, the lessons learned, and the inspirations gathered, knowing that these elements will continue to shape your future travels and enrich your life's journey.

8.2 Final Tips and Farewell

As your journey through Ireland comes to a close, it's time to gather the wisdom and insights that will enrich your travel experiences for years to come. Every adventure leaves a mark, and the Emerald Isle, with its lush landscapes and vibrant culture, has likely imparted a wealth of memories and lessons. Here, we'll explore some final tips to ensure that your travels remain not only enjoyable but also meaningful and fulfilling.

One of the most valuable aspects of travel is the opportunity to connect with the local culture. Ireland is renowned for its warm hospitality and welcoming spirit. Engaging with locals can offer profound insights into the country's way of life and traditions. Whether it's sharing stories with a friendly pub-goer or participating in a local festival, these interactions can deepen your understanding and appreciation of the places you visit. Make a conscious effort to step out of your comfort zone and embrace these connections—they often lead to the most memorable experiences.

As you travel, remember the importance of being a responsible and respectful visitor. This extends to the environment, the people, and the cultural heritage of each destination. Ireland's landscapes are fragile and require mindful exploration. Stay on designated paths and leave no trace behind to preserve the natural beauty for future travelers. When visiting historical sites, respect the guidelines and regulations in place to protect these irreplaceable treasures. By practicing responsible tourism, you contribute to the preservation of Ireland's heritage and natural wonders.

Embrace the spontaneity that travel often brings. While having a plan is essential, some of the best travel experiences arise from unplanned moments. Allow yourself the freedom to deviate from itineraries and explore off-the-beaten-path locations. These spontaneous adventures can lead to unique discoveries, whether it's a hidden beach, a quaint village, or a breathtaking viewpoint. Keep an open mind and a flexible schedule to make the most of these opportunities.

Food is a gateway to understanding a culture, and Ireland's culinary scene has much to offer. From hearty traditional dishes to innovative modern cuisine, each meal is a chance to explore the flavors and ingredients that define the region. Don't shy away from trying new foods, whether it's a classic Irish stew or a freshly caught seafood dish. Visit local markets to sample artisanal products and engage with the producers who take pride in their craft. These culinary experiences are a feast for the senses and offer a deeper connection to the lands you traverse.

Documenting your journey through writing, photography, or art can enhance your travel experience and preserve memories for the future. Keeping a travel journal allows you to reflect on daily experiences, capturing thoughts and emotions that might otherwise fade over time. Photography offers a visual narrative of your travels, enabling you to share the beauty and diversity of Ireland with others. Artistic endeavors, such as sketching or painting, encourage you to observe your surroundings more closely, fostering a deeper appreciation for the details of each place.

As your journey concludes, take the time to reflect on the growth and learning that travel brings. Each adventure offers lessons in adaptability, patience, and understanding. Traveling challenges preconceived notions and broadens perspectives, ultimately contributing to personal development. Consider how your experiences in Ireland have influenced your views and aspirations. Use these reflections as a foundation for future travels, guiding you towards new horizons and deeper connections.

Finally, as you bid farewell to Ireland, hold onto the friendships and connections you've made along the way. Whether it's fellow travelers or local hosts, these relationships form a network of shared experiences and memories. Stay in touch with those who have enriched your journey, and perhaps find ways to return the hospitality and kindness you've received. These connections transcend borders, reminding us of the shared humanity that unites us all.

Travel is a journey of discovery, both outward and inward. As you leave the Emerald Isle, carry with you the beauty, stories, and lessons that have unfolded along the way. Let them inspire future adventures and enrich your understanding of the world. In every journey, whether near or far, the spirit of exploration and discovery lives on, inviting you to continue seeking the wonders that lie beyond the horizon.

BONUS 1: ESSENTIAL PHRASES FOR YOUR DAILY TRAVEL NEEDS IN IRELAND

BONUS 2: PRINTABLE TRAVEL JOURNAL